Change Your Story, Change Your Life

Rewrite the Past and Live an Empowered Now!

Beatrice Elliott

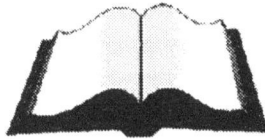

CCB Publishing
British Columbia, Canada

Change Your Story, ChangeYour Life: Rewrite the Past and
Live an Empowered Now!

Copyright ©2007 by Beatrice Elliott
ISBN-13 978-0-9784388-2-1
First Edition

Library and Archives Canada Cataloguing in Publication
Elliott, Beatrice, 1946-
Change Your Story, Change Your Life: Rewrite the Past and Live an
Empowered Now! / written by Beatrice Elliott.
Also available in electronic format.
ISBN 978-0-9784388-2-1
1. Self-actualization (Psychology). I. Title.
BF637.S4E46 2007   158.1   C2007-906413-2

Cover design by Joan Doyle: www.theHouseArtist.com
Jasper & Zephyr illustration by Jon William Lopez:
www.enlightimages.com
All other images contained herein are considered public domain and are
reproduced without malice.

Publisher: CCB Publishing
              British Columbia, Canada
              www.ccbpublishing.com

I dedicate this book to my real life "Power Posse"…

Mary Bullard, who has 92 years of inspiration. I thank her for her love, interest and being my proverbial cheerleader.

Also to my son, Elliott Kuhn, who has been my consistent supporter for all my creative projects.
I want him to know how much his wonderful creativity has been an inspiration for my own.

Other books by Beatrice Elliott

Perfect Praying:
5 Simple Steps That Make Prayers Work
(co-authored with Jon William Lopez)

Foreword

I have always been a lover of stories. I think, if having to choose between food and fable, I would be very hard pressed to pick the obvious. Growing up in an over-populated clan of Irish Gypsies, I was raised on stories, tales and folklore. Of all the characters to ever manifest in the theater of my mind via the words of some wonderful storyteller, the one that I most related to was the little child in the *Emperor's New Clothes* who pointed out the simple yet seemingly manipulated truth, that the King was indeed naked. I loved this child and this story for the same reasons that I love Bea Elliott and her wonderful book *Change Your Story, Change Your Life.*

Although the whole world was trapped in an illusion, the child stayed fully rooted in the truth and was able to set the whole village free. Yes, "the truth will set you free," and yet the truth can be so subjective. There is my truth and the parking attendant's truth, there is our truth and their truth and never the twain shall meet. Until now, that is. Bea Elliott is a truth worker and the path that she has paved for us is a wonderful journey of resurrection that will reveal and heal illusions of separation and dis-ease and lead the reader to understanding, forgiveness and enlightenment.

Many years ago, I had the fortune of taking a workshop entitled "From Wound to Wisdom." At the time this student was ready, the teacher appeared, and it was Bea. Under her guidance, I was able bring to light old stories that had kept me in old beliefs, beliefs that no longer served me. I began to see how these unexamined stories of my past kept me running on a hamster wheel. It was bittersweet to acknowledge the fact that I had been wearing the ruby slippers all along.

The truth is: the past does not have to be set in stone. Through working these simple exercises and examining these questions you can begin to restructure your stories, and thereby redirect your life.

I think another good title for this book may have been "Bea, Not Afraid." For it is from Bea Elliott's courage to examine the many faces of Truth that we all have the opportunity to benefit. She is the child who continues to challenge us to take another look, see a greater possibility and be open to a new actuality. As you begin your journey, I encourage you to "be not afraid," for greater peace and freedom awaits you.

Maureen Muldoon, RScP
Creator/Director "Booby Trap"
Actress TV and Film

Preface

Pondering over a warm cup of coffee on a brisk fall morning a few years back, I wondered what I would have been like if my parents had gone through their divorce differently. You know, without the badmouthing and blaming. Divorce has a way of absorbing the two adults in the emotional crisis, often disallowing a space for the children's feelings. I wondered how I might have experienced my subsequent relationships with friends, lovers and husbands. Perhaps I would have done better in sharing my feelings in those relationships if my parents had asked me from time to time, "What are you feeling about this divorce? What are your needs? Is there something you want to say to us?"

The idea came to me to rewrite that dismal time and have it play out differently. I wanted to rewrite a particular crisis as a storybook and bring with me an adult point of view and new choices that I didn't have access to as a 15-year-old girl.

Being a parent myself and an educator, I loved reading stories to children that had imaginary "do-gooder" characters, real crusaders for the child. I decided to rewrite my history and include two imaginary friends: Jasper the Joybird and Zephyr the Wind. This dynamic duo would time travel back with me to direct and inspire the younger me.

I put pen to paper to rewrite a specific incident with my father. I recalled how I physically looked, described details of the house I was living in and how I was feeling about my life. I wrote down the questions I asked myself because they seemed to bring me back to the emotional colors of that particular time.

As I conjured up all the sensory detail, I found myself not just thinking about the incident from a remote perspective, but actually living through it again. Only this time, I had my "Power Posse" of Jasper and Zephyr to guide me in rewriting my story. Jasper served as my confidante, encouraging me to let loose all my feelings. He was the problem solver, informing me of more empowering choices. I cast Zephyr as the illuminator. He helped me understand my part in the bigger picture, inspired me to release old emotions and move towards understanding and forgiveness.

I also wanted to address in my rewritten story the mind/body connection to aid in healing. I had suffered from Epstein-Barr Virus in the 1980's and breast cancer in the 1990's. I definitely sensed that my mental and emotional state was adversely affecting my physical health. I read Louise Hay's books, which clearly explained the emotional causes linked to physical disease or "dis-ease." I decided to include this aspect in my story by giving Jasper a rainbow-colored tail, which represented the colors of the seven charkas, or energy systems, of the body. Our emotions are often locked in one or many of the chakras. In my story, Jasper presents my child self with a tail feather that represents the appropriate color of the affected chakra: a green feather to heal my heart.

Having cast all the characters and asked myself the difficult questions, I began writing my personal parable, *Bea Wished*. I tried not to think and just let myself write. I gave myself permission to feel pent up emotions I had never fully explored before. Spurred on by Jasper, I let them go and made empowering choices. Zephyr gently suggested I view the antagonist with more compassionate eyes, so I could release the stress of false perception. My story flowed out of me all the way to a different and more empowering ending.

I felt clear. It was a catharsis with a difference. This process revealed new insights. It felt fun doing this rewriting with my personal "Power Posse" at my side for support and direction. The two imaginary characters were the true voice of my heart, a voice that had been muted by the chatter of my mind's limited perception and disabling beliefs.

The *re-storying* gave me distance from the painful childhood event; instead I immersed myself in the positive thoughts and actions of the heroic characters. I felt *re-stored*. I experienced even more healing as I shared my story with loved ones. They said listening to my story helped them to understand me better. A few months after rewriting my story, I experienced shifts in my perceptions and changes in my personal relationships. I communicated more clearly with my partner at the time and felt more comfortable in my own skin. Later, I rewrote my story again as part of my process of healing breast cancer. I have since healed my body and am disease free.

Seeing a change in me, friends and clients asked me to guide them through the same process. They, too, experienced a sense of release and closure. Later, they reported positive effects in their lives as well. These stories had a purpose: to heal the heart and reveal the truth that we are all whole, perfect and complete.

Chapter one discusses psychological, metaphysical and spiritual theories behind storytelling as a healing modality. In chapter two, I explain how I discovered Jasper and Zephyr and allow the characters to introduce themselves to the reader. In chapter three, I share with you my story, *Bea Wished*. In subsequent chapters, I share some of my clients' stories. Each chapter begins with a brief background of the person's life and concludes with the shifts that have occurred since the story was rewritten. The workbook section, *Now It's Your Turn*, is a user-friendly guide for rewriting your own story, using my characters or your own. Even if you've never written anything before, you can rewrite your story and right your life. May you enjoy the process of opening your life to all its inner riches.

Bea Elliott
Studio City, California, 2007

Contents

Introduction

What if you could go back to your childhood and delete any experiences and reactions that began to distort your self perception? What if you could go back without hours of self analysis, inventories and endless questionnaires which comprise most current self help books? What if this discovery process actually featured a fun filled fantasy with wit, wisdom and whimsy? What if you really began to FEEL rather than THINK how these changes could make a difference in your life?

Change Your Story, Change Your Life intends to do just that. The dynamic duo of Jasper the Joybird and Zephyr the Wind time travel with you back to your childhood to rewrite a wrong. Many people spend much time in therapy, 12-step programs and expanding their self help libraries. Yet they still don't take that 12-inch trip from their head to their heart.

If we look at the great Teachers of our times, Jesus or Buddha, they knew the value of parables. Storytelling plays a major part in many aspects of our culture, as seen in movies, television and novels. However we totally ignore the value of this tool when applying it to the discovery of our true self. This book uses the fantasy of storytelling, combined with the support of two loveable characters, Jasper and Zephyr, to rewrite stories of adult remembrances of a painful childhood event. The stories create new internal reactions to this situation, which replace the old false negative beliefs.

These stories, which are thematically organized, i.e. divorce, bully victim, abandonment, etc., are universal in their topics and appeal. As the story plays out with wit and whimsy and always much wisdom, the reader sees the value of rewriting their own story. The book ends with just that opportunity. The final chapters entitled *Now It's Your Turn* and *Writing Your Own Personal Parable* invite the reader to think of their own past incident which they would like to rewrite. They are easily led through a concise questionnaire that brings forth the emotional and visual details of that earlier time to be incorporated into their story.

There are story prompts that begin the co-creating process, i.e "Jasper is sailing high above the earth enjoying the soft breath of his best friend, Zephyr. As Jasper looks down, he sees... " (Describe the outside location as clearly as possible. Use words that paint the picture.)

To digress, it is important to mention that beyond the purpose of re-pairing the mind with the truth of the heart, these stories have an additional mission of aligning the body's energy systems as well. It is becoming well accepted in western medicine that stress, depression and anxiety take their toll on the human body and delete years from one's life. Andrew Weil, M.D. has been a forerunner in touting the need to master our emotions for our own personal quality of life.

Emotions are stored in the body's energy systems, also known as chakras, and blocking the flow of this energy can lead to physical ailments. Changing the stories changes the emotions felt in the past, which lead to more empowering self beliefs. There is a visceral reaction, a release of the distorted reality and a restoring of our natural energy flow. We begin to vibrate at a higher energy level and we attract more good into our lives. We are what we believe.

Jasper has a beautiful rainbow-colored tail which is color coded to the seven chakra energy systems. The theme of the story dictates the color of the beautiful feather that Jasper gives to the main character, along with a corresponding chakra affirmation. There is a concise chakra chart at the end of the book so the reader can see each chakra lesson, physical area and emotional component. As you'll see, these stories are not only entertaining, but are also brimming with transformational opportunities for the reader at the level of mind, body and heart.

Chapter One

Story as Medicine

The Power of the Parable

Do you remember the stories of your childhood?

I bet you do. Whether the stories were old fairy tales or Disney movies or Uncle George recounting how he eloped with Aunt Freda, these stories resonated with you long after they were experienced.

We didn't know it then, but even simple stories about a rabbit or a bear or a frog helped us connect to a deeper part of ourselves. We fell in love with a particular character, perhaps one that represented the qualities we wanted to embrace in ourselves. A shaggy dog courageously exposes a cat that wrongfully blamed him for eating his master's dinner, when, in real life, we were too afraid to confront a sister who wrongfully accused us. A little mouse traps the bully cat in his own trap, when, in real life, our next door neighbor Sam was taunting us with punches in the stomach. We didn't have the adult perspective to define why we felt good after absorbing a story into our being. We just felt good.

While we know that not all endings are happy in real life, the happy ending of those childhood stories helped us to transcend our childhood suffering and bring a new perspective to our experience. The stories helped to change the emotional emphasis of our traumatic experience from feeling hopeless to resolve it, to feeling empowered at having directly confronted the beast. Although the sister and the bully next door may have continued to wreak havoc on our young psyches, through these stories that were embedded into our unconscious, we felt the possibility of a different ending inside. We felt the possibility of a larger, fuller life.

As a child, my love of stories went beyond books and movies. My mother entertained me by recounting simple stories of her childhood, living on a wheat farm in Idaho. The youngest sister of a big Norwegian family of five sisters and four brothers, my mother loved to watch her older sisters get dressed up for formal college balls. As she described in detail the gowns they wore, I could picture everything she told me. As if peering into a window of my own future with men, I was fascinated with the drama of the dating games they played. I begged for more stories.

I wanted to be enveloped in the world of story. My grandmother, who lived on a ranch in the woods of Northern California, read us pages of *Swiss Family Robinson* during our summers with her. My brother and I were so enthralled with the idea of a family living in a tree house that we created a makeshift replica in the forest and pretended to be the Robinsons. We *lived* the story.

By the third grade of my Catholic school education, I began to write and illustrate my own comic strips. I felt a deep fulfillment in writing the words and drawing the images of my characters, much to the chagrin of the nun, who said in front of class, that my heroine, dressed in a strapless gown, was inappropriately attired. But it wasn't until years later as an adult that I discovered why creating my own stories was so satisfying.

As an adult, I have learned that simple storytelling can have a powerful affect on how we integrate our experiences. Recently, I attended a workshop led by Jonathan Young, Ph.D., who years before assisted famous mythologist Joseph Campbell for several years at seminars. During the workshop, Dr. Young told the story of *The Ugly Duckling*. It was a story that I'd heard as a child many times, but this time I experienced such a profound connection to hearing the story. I realized that I still felt the same feelings in response to the story as when I was a little girl. Only now, as an adult, I caught so much more of the nuances in meaning. Most importantly, I felt like I was still that ugly duckling that was in the process of discovering she was a beautiful swan. I was still that little girl inside.

In working with clients as a spiritual counselor for many years, I discovered that the little girl or boy we once were, is still very much inside us all and not far from the surface of our lives. Yet it is not a part of ourselves that we consciously pay attention to. We are too busy trying to keep up with the information overload, the work and family schedules, the trips to the doctor for the annoying ailments that just won't go away. How can we possibly pay attention to our inner child's longings when the sink is stopped up, the bills are overdue and our own child is tugging at our arm to get him a cookie?

That child part of us is very much alive in our unconscious minds. Our dreams speak to us in a language the child understands: through mythical and fantastical stories. We may dream of dragons or earthquakes or some unidentifiable terror chasing us, but that could be our unconscious speaking to us about our troubled relationship with our spouse. The unconscious memories jarred during the day from simply hearing a familiar piece of music or breathing in a voluptuous scent, can appear as a dramatic story as we sleep. Just when we think we have contained our conscious experience of reality in a neat little box, out pops a trickster like a jack-in-the-box to remind us of what disturbances need addressing on a deeper level. We don't always want to look at the feelings that seem inconvenient to deal with, but the unconscious mind has a way of nagging us to face what we haven't yet integrated into our lives. It's easy for many of us to view our dreams as meaningless entertainment and forget about them. But if we are to truly heal and discover the truth about ourselves, we need to pay attention to these messages from the unconscious.

In listening intimately to my clients, I have found that a problem that has been recurring in their lives is often directly related to a traumatic experience in their childhood. One client found out that the present situation of a boss overlooking her for a promotion evoked the same overwhelming emotions as when, at age seven, she was the last to be picked on a soccer team. She cried, feeling the pain all over again of that seven year old girl inside of her. This experience with her boss only reinforced what she had come to believe about herself: that no matter how hard she worked, she could not measure up.

What we believe about ourselves is the foggy filter of how we experience everything that happens to us. So, uncovering our core beliefs is vital to clearing the way towards the direction of happiness and fulfillment. Whether or not we consciously remember our early experiences, they remain with us and color our beliefs about ourselves. Yet it is a precarious process of developing these beliefs about ourselves. What we remember is a subjective interpretation of what we experienced and not necessarily the objective truth of the situation. We may judge our experiences as good or bad, joyful or painful. If we never go back and review these memories, we may stay stuck in beliefs and behavior patterns that no longer serve us. Our present life may be playing out these outdated stories, resulting in a fatalistic feeling that our lives will never be different. Unless we purposely revisit these stories, we will never be free to live from our truthful core. But when we do revisit them, the possibilities of our life abound again. Our dreams can give us hints at what is really going on inside of us, but we can take a more active role in reviewing the messages of our unconscious by recreating an early traumatic experience through storytelling. By going back as adults into our child self to review these experiences, we not only see our past from a different perspective, but we see how the past connects to our current concerns. By "restory-ing" our childhood experiences, we consciously "re-store" ourselves to who we really are, free from the stifling box of self-limiting beliefs.

It can feel like a daunting adventure to return to those painful memories. After I'd experienced heartbreaks in my relationships with men, I sensed that this pattern might be connected to my experience of my parents' divorce. I decided to write about my recollection of this time. But I felt ambivalent about bringing up the past and the painful feelings of how I felt my needs were invisible to my father. I decided that I needed to find a way of rewriting the stories of my past, in a safer, more approachable way. When my parents were going through their bitter divorce, I remembered thinking it would be great to have an invisible animal friend on my side that I could tell all my feelings to. I decided to re-story a particular incident during that time by using storybook characters to guide me through the experience. And so Jasper the Joybird and Zephyr the Wind were cast.

With Jasper the Joybird coaxing me to express what I was really feeling in the moment and take positive action, I felt an inner strength to face my feelings and speak my needs to my father in my rewritten story. With Zephyr the Wind providing a balanced and wise perspective, I could see a larger picture of what happened then and could choose how to feel about the experience. This "Power Posse" was giving voice to my wise, loving self and replacing my overdeveloped inner critic! With the help of these guides, I could see my father as the imperfect yet loving man that he was. And I could see myself as the courageous heroine of my own story who created a different and triumphant outcome by expressing her needs and realizing that she was valued and loved.

Seeing myself in that way had a magnificent impact on my self-esteem and the way I related to friends and loved ones. I felt a different vibration and as a Spiritual Counselor, I knew that it was from this point that I would attract new conditions into my life. I realized that I had stumbled on to what the ancients had been practicing for centuries: the power of storytelling to heal and bring meaning to our lives. Without going back, replacing the old feeling with a new one, we cannot go as far forward.

Without remembering our past and self-reflecting, we cannot fully see ourselves and live from our larger truth in the present. As a child we thought our perceptions were absolutely the truth about ourselves. However when we become adults, if we don't go back and explore those situations with our adult consciousness and discover a more positive belief, we keep attracting from the old, limiting belief.

It is in recounting our pasts that we have a chance to review how we arrived at our beliefs. I discovered through re-storying my life that besides the healing power of remembering, it is in having an active role in creating new beliefs about ourselves that propels our self-healing to a higher level. I saw the connection of rewriting my story with the principles I'd been studying as a Practitioner in the Church of Religious Science.

The Church of Religious Science, or Science of Mind, was founded circa 1927 by Dr. Ernest Holmes, a self-taught philosopher who studied all the spiritual paths and discovered a powerful synthesis of the working principles in all religions. Science of Mind is based on the theory that there is One Infinite Mind which includes all that there is. It teaches how to use the Mind Principle for helping ourselves and others to overcome problems such as despair, poverty and sickness.

The Science of Mind defines the highest potential of each human being by stating that everyone has inherent God-like qualities within. Each of us is a co-creator with the Divine. It is this divinely creative capacity of our true nature that enables us to create a life for ourselves that is completely fulfilling in its every aspect. But it starts with identifying our objective circumstances as originally stemming from the quality of our thoughts.

The Science of Mind describes negative consequences as stemming from wrong thought which leads to wrong belief. We believe that in order to have positive changes in our life, we need to change our thoughts about how much good we can experience. We believe that in changing our thought's stream of consciousness, we can produce a corresponding change in our environments. The Science of Mind technique for change is based on thinking right thoughts, which leads to right beliefs and behaviors which then produce the right conditions in our life. This is also known as the Law of Attraction.

By re-storying our lives, we are going back into our pasts and feeling how we experienced a traumatic incident; we can often find the root of a belief that has grown into a tree in our adult lives, whether for good or bad effect. Part of the task of discovery is to ask ourselves specific questions about the incident, so that we can find the thoughts and beliefs behind the actions and feelings. These questions have been included in the workbook section at the end of this book. Since each of us experiences our lives through the filter of these long-held beliefs, we can see how our stories have influenced our self-esteem, ethics, work life, relationships, values and spiritual life. By having swallowed these childhood beliefs whole, they have become a part of our cells. We think this is the reality of life, when in fact we have just created a *story* about reality of which we are living proof. Through rewriting our stories, we can now choose new choices to counter our negative beliefs and replace them with the positive thoughts and actions of the heroes and heroines of our story: ourselves.

We can also go a step further and observe the thoughts, feelings and beliefs we hold of our friends and loved ones. How much has our belief about the "bad guy or girl" in our stories continued to limit our perception of this person and keep us stuck in an estranged relationship? Or how much of our negative belief have we passed on to our own children? The "sins of the father" syndrome can be played out subconsciously. This is a big motivator to get straight with ourselves, isn't it? As we are restored to the truth of ourselves and learn to love ourselves unconditionally, we can then bring that generosity to our relationships with others. I found that through rewriting my own story, I was able to move beyond blame and powerlessness to forgiving my parents and embracing them, as whole and complete, despite their weaknesses. I was able to pass that type of positive thinking on to my son. He could see that his Mom and Dad weren't perfect either, but really only human, doing the best we could with what we had at the time. He was able to arrive at this conclusion after reading my story. This is another real gift of rewriting your story and sharing it with your kids, they can discover your pearls of wisdom themselves.

In the workbook section you will be asked questions that prompt memories of your past. As we return to those early experiences and rewrite them, we can often see the connection of the past filtered experience and how we continue to use the same filters in similar circumstances in the present. With this new perspective of our past, we can then choose to process information in the present in a healthier, more informed way.

Our values help us decide what is good or bad, right or wrong. We make judgments about ourselves based on these values, so it's important to identify what our values are, and their hierarchy of priorities. Our values are the result of our internal model of the world. If our model of the world differs from our values or someone else's, there's conflict.

Beliefs are what we have presupposed about the world. They can either empower us or destroy us. The important task in re-storying our past, is to find out the disabling beliefs that get in the way of the magnificence of who we really are and attaining true and lasting happiness and success. Our memories are responsible for coloring our present and our presence.

By rewriting our stories, we have a chance to explore the language, images and feelings that encompass our experience. We can then choose to open our perception beyond our filters to see a larger and more empowering story.

By modeling a successful person, we can apply this element of modeling in rewriting our stories with ourselves as the heroic character. If we have been teased by other children because we are dyslexic, we can go back and choose a different way to respond to the teasing. We can even take our actions a step further and make friends of our tormentors by educating them about dyslexia.

Another way to rewrite your story is to embody positive traits in other characters that represent different empowering parts of the self, as has been done with the characters Jasper the Joybird and Zephyr the Wind. For instance, in the childhood incident I rewrote as *Bea Wished*, which I present in chapter three, I couldn't ask for the understanding and reassurance I needed from my father, who was consumed by his own sadness during a difficult divorce. But Jasper and Zephyr encouraged me to take the steps to get my needs met. Zephyr represents the voice of my higher wisdom, so that I could see that despite my father's self-absorption, he really loved and valued me. Jasper represents my empowered self that takes positive action to be heard and get my needs met.

Is there someone that you respect and admire and would like to emulate? We can incorporate this person's belief system, mental syntax (the way a person organizes information) and physiology into our childhood character. By going back into the childhood incident as the empowered child with an informed adult perception, we can experience the incident anew, using all our senses to filter the experience in a more positive way. When you rewrite your story, project these qualities in your own personal wise guides; you are not locked into using Jasper and Zephyr.

We have discussed the importance of understanding our

beliefs and the way we filter information, but we haven't addressed the very important element of our physiology. The stories locked in our unconscious not only affect our memory, belief systems and the way we filter our present experience, but they can live in our bodies. A friend of mine who is a body worker includes the following slogan on her business card, "Our issues are in our tissues." We are living out the decisions we made in childhood about who we are and the possibilities and limitations of our lives. These unconscious decisions and beliefs have also affected our physical health. Often, re-storying our early experiences can help us restore our bodies as well.

The Mind/Body Connection and the Chakra System

Have you ever awoken from a dream of falling off a cliff? Do you remember how your breath quickened and your heart beat furiously? The fact is our bodies don't know the difference between an imagined event and a real one. Conversely, if we had a pleasant dream of swimming in a tropical island lagoon, we can feel peace and relaxation as we wake up to greet the day. Stories have the same powerful effect. Other cultures know the power of storytelling and give it due respect as a healing modality. In Islamic societies, loved ones tell a sick person an uplifting story. It helps the sick person imagine their own triumph over circumstances, which then empowers the immune system to heal the body.

Hindu physicians employ fairy tales to help emotionally troubled patients because they understand their mysteriously powerful effect on the subconscious.

Because of my own struggles with Epstein-Barr Virus and

breast cancer, I felt it was crucial to address the connection of my emotions and beliefs to my physical health. As I began to study books on the mind/body connection, I saw examples of how certain beliefs based on childhood experiences positively or adversely affected physical health years later. It seemed that going back to rewrite these childhood traumas might also improve our health as well as our attitudes. I incorporated into my story the ancient Indian system of the chakras and gave Jasper a rainbow-colored tail of feathers representing each of seven chakras.

Chakra means "wheel." Chakras are energy centers or vortices. They are used to understand the way energy is processed by the human being. The "Lower Triangle" chakras focus on elimination and reduction and are balanced by the "Upper Triangle" chakras which accumulate, create and refine. The fourth chakra, the heart chakra is the balance between the two, where we experience shifts from "me to we." A seventh chakra represents the aura or magnetic field of the body. It is said that cosmic energy flows down from the eighth chakra and collects in the other chakras. The chakras affect our perceptions, feelings and choices. They affect the flow and types of thoughts we have. They affect the relationship between the conscious and the subconscious. There are many practices and healing modalities, such as yoga, Tai Chi, acupuncture, etc. that address balancing the energy of the chakras and clearing blockages that lead to mental, emotional and physical distress.

Each chakra has a particular location in the body and has organs and glands associated with it. There are positive qualities of each chakra when balanced and negative qualities when they're out of balance. For instance, the first chakra, or root chakra, is located at the end of the spine between the anus and sexual organs. It concerns security and survival issues and governs the organs of elimination. The color associated with this chakra is red. The positive qualities of this chakra are a feeling of being grounded, security, stability, loyalty and healthy bodily functions of elimination. When out of balance, we feel fear and insecurity. Life can feel like a burden. We can feel out of touch with our families or culture. Physically there are problems with a weak constitution, elimination problems and lowered resistance. In the Appendix a chakra chart has been included for your reference, which identifies each of the chakras and their qualities.

When rewriting our stories, it's important to pay attention to how you feel in your body. How does it feel in your gut? If you were hurt physically, where was the wound? Did you feel grounded in your body during the experience, or were you in your head? By re-experiencing the emotions associated with the event, we can often find the reactive patterns in our body that stem from those emotions. Feeling an emotion in a certain chakra can also give you insights into the unconscious issues associated with that chakra that need addressing.

In my own case, it was no wonder that the accumulated hurts and emotional pain I'd experienced caused an imbalance in my heart chakra, which then manifested as breast cancer. During my recovery I attended a breast cancer support group and the psychologist leading the group asked me if I knew the profile of women who experienced breast cancer. I replied that I did not. He informed me that these women were very competent about taking care of other people's feelings but not as competent in taking care of their own. Hmm, I definitely identified with this group. Therefore, I decided to approach my recovery with the best of western and alternative medicine, while addressing the emotional and spiritual causes of such a disease. As part of my treatment, I chose to rewrite my *Bea Wished* story again. This time, I delved deeper into the experience than before and concentrated on what I felt in my Heart Chakra. The Heart Chakra rules subtle feelings and the ability to touch others with our purity of feeling. It is also about boundaries, both on the physical and emotional levels. When it functions well, it knows how to discern when something is foreign and needs to be examined, versus when something is a part of you and can be accepted in. It can also help you determine what people are worthy to enter your heart space and when to protect your boundaries. In rewriting my story about feeling abandoned because of my father's emotional absence, I allowed myself to feel kindness towards him and the possibility of his warmth and love in the moments I most needed them. I started to feel my heart opening. I could feel that the healing taking place in my emotional heart was also healing my breasts.

During that time, I also discovered another avenue of healing: sharing our stories with each other. When we are really listened to, we feel cared for, respected and heard.

When we really listen to one another, we are actively and creatively engaged in opening ourselves to new places, people and experiences. We give our energy to the storyteller and can even heal the storyteller through our loving attention.

Family Story Sharing

When you, as a family, share your stories with each other and by asking each other "what can we learn from this?" you are encouraged to draw your own conclusions and consider how the story feels to you. The story then becomes a lesson that you can use in your lives. I encourage you to dive into the workbook section and give yourself and your family the gift of exploring the depth and richness of your inner world.

There was a time, as a society, when we gathered together to share stories. Storytelling was a nightly event that helped to synthesize and bring meaning to the events of the day. Now we live in a world that feeds us constant information via media which keeps us isolated from human interaction. Yet we still are famished for the words that would deliver a deeper connection to our experience of the world, of each other, of ourselves. By getting in touch with our own life stories, we offer to ourselves and each other the possibility of deeper, shared understanding, compassion and the possibility of a true and lasting experience of peace.

How to Benefit from this Book

I would like to suggest that you first read the stories. Each story gives you a brief synopsis of the adult whose story you are about to read. Of course, the name and locations have been changed to protect their anonymity. If you have children or grandchildren, read the stories together and discuss what they would do in the same situation, and if anything like that has ever happened to them. You will find out a lot about each other's thinking. Share the story with your partner and the same revelations will take place. By reading the stories first, you will get a good feel of the positive voices that you will want to incorporate into your own personal parable.

In the part of the book, *Now It's Your Turn*, the questionnaire will ask you thought provoking questions that will bring up past incidents that are ripe for reworking. These incidents can be from your childhood or any part of your past that you would like to revisit and to rewrite. Find a quiet space that is free of distractions and where you can be alone. I would suggest stopping here, but if you feel like you are on a roll, move into the *Writing Your Own Personal Parable* section and begin rewriting your story. You will probably revise your story several times. This is a loving process, so be gentle with yourself. It will take as long as it takes. Journal your dreams after writing your story, as many insights can appear. Observe your life situations in the six months after writing your story and note what changes are taking place. I suggest sharing your story with a loved one, and be sure you let the person know up front if you want feedback or for them just to listen. Share your story with children; they are so attuned to stories, and to think that this is your true story just makes you that much more real to them. It also gives them permission to share incidents that are currently going on in their lives. I hope that your family can begin to share their personal stories with each other at family gatherings; think of the small talk that will be replaced with transformative dialogue. Have fun making covers for your stories and keeping them as a family memoir to be passed on from generation to generation. Now good healthy perceptions can be passed on rather than the old limiting beliefs.

My wish for you is to enjoy this process, to gain a new life enhancing perspective of the true you, and to have your life attract all that you know it so richly deserves. Of course, being an educator, I want you to also remember to share your story with a child; you are remembering your past, while they are actively living it in the present. Let's all rewrite our stories so our children can live a healthier NOW.

Chapter Two

Meet the Power Posse – Jasper & Zephyr

In the stories that you are about to read in the following chapters, I've created a dynamic duo to journey back with the main character in each story. They are the "Power Posse" for the central character and will be there to cheer her/him and to empower her/him with new and more effective choices. The characters utilized are a talking bird, Jasper the Joybird, and his best friend, Zephyr the Wind. I've pondered why I chose a bird and wind for my stories, and then upon closer examination discovered that they are in fact perfect metaphors for these healing stories. Zephyr symbolizes the unseen Wisdom that is always present in each of us and Jasper is the manifestation of the Joy we can see when we are aligned and acting from this Source.

Actually the idea of Jasper and Zephyr was germinated when my good college friend, Charlotte, and I were talking one evening when she mentioned that she had just visited some friends who had a truly amazing talking bird named Jasper. The conversation began taking on a life of its own as we began to get philosophical about our feathered friends. Charlotte said tongue in cheek that she always thought birds must be the great communicators on this planet as they are privy to all our conversations and information when they are sitting on the telephone wires. I suggested that it would be fun if we had a talking bird as our wise friend that could come down and help with our problems. Charlotte added that the bird should have a friend, noting that the name Zephyr had come to her recently in a dream. I thought that was a perfect team. I further suggested giving this team a mission, and once they had accepted the mission, whenever they came upon a problem Jasper would lose elevation and have to come down to earth and help the distressed person. We concluded our conversation and felt very happy about our new imaginary friends.

These little friends sat on a shelf somewhere in my consciousness and were resurrected when I began my spiritual counseling. I used Jasper and Zephyr as the Power Posse in the stories that I was rewriting for my clients. It helped to have these characters and the story format, and then to wrap the client's personal stories around them. I subsequently found out that the stone Jasper is also referred to as the healing stone. Hmm, what a coincidence, or not!

When writing your own personal story using the tools provided in this book, you can use Japer and Zephyr or you can make up your own Power Posse as your support team. The characters are not what's important, but rather their supportive, compassionate voices.

During a workshop on this subject one male participant remarked that he could not relate to a talking bird for his rewritten story. I asked him to whom he could relate, and he said that Joseph Campbell was one of his personal heroes. So I said, "Tell Joseph to pack his bags, you're taking him on a little trip." Be creative! If Jasper and Zephyr don't work for you, create your own; *you* are the casting agent for this story, so this can also be a fun endeavor. This is where you give permission to your imagination to work full throttle. I love the quote "Imagination is more important than Intelligence" by Albert Einstein. I believe he is someone we would agree knew what he was talking about, right?

Having said this I would like to introduce you to Jasper and Zephyr and their story line:

Jasper the Joybird surrounded by his friend, Zephyr the Wind

Jasper: Hi, I'm Jasper the JoyBird – Welcome to Stories that Reveal Your Truth and Heal Your Heart. I love to fly in the air and enjoy life just like you. I have a wonderfully wise friend, Zephyr the Wind. Say hi, Zephyr.

Zephyr: *Welcome fellow journeyers.*

Jasper: Zeph's a little heavy, but he really has some great insights to share, so just bare with him. As I said, I love wind surfing, a little air backstroke and a thrilling loop-de-loop. How carefree can one little bird be? Oh and check out my rainbow-colored tail feathers… pretty snazzy, eh? I'll tell you more about them later. Well these stories that follow aren't about me and Zephyr, they're about real adults! How so? Well let me explain. We have been cast in the story to give them a happier and more empowering spin. We're Spiritual Spin Doctors you might say. This is how it works. Each story features an adult's remembrance of a past situation that really left them hurting. The event has really stuck with them and caused them to form a belief about themselves that is still keeping them from operating at their full potential. These stories focus on experiences such as, divorce, betrayal, abandonment; you know, all the stuff that we experience here on earth. In each story Zephyr and I help the person to make different choices that will make for a happier ending. The last chapter of the book is going to be your turn. You tell your story by filling out the questionnaire and following the story prompts and voila, you have your own personalized Jasper the Joybird story.

Zephyr: *You know what's amazing? When we see our remembrance redone in story form, we begin to feel the emotions that the story evokes. We get to feel what that new empowering ending brings up for us. We feel our good through the story. We are helped to see the choices that were available to us but not apparent at the time.*

Jasper: Thanks, Zephyr. Let me demonstrate the format of our stories. Every story begins with Zephyr and I joyously traveling the world high up in the blue sky. However we have a contract with the Universe that wherever there is a hurting heart, our contract is activated and we must come to assist.

It plays out like this: I flap and flap and Zephyr blows and blows, but to no avail. I lose elevation and land kerplunk – back to earth. We now know a new adventure is about to begin. I look around and sure enough we see you in the past and we witness your problem. What we love is that we know you already know the right thing to do, so our story merely helps point out the choices available to you.

Zephyr: *An un-mended past hurt remains alive in an adult heart.*

Jasper: Exactly! When we step up to the plate to support you, a new healthier memory replaces the old one. Simple, but powerful! Oh, and these tail feathers are not just rainbow-colored for the fun of it. Nope, each one represents one of the seven energy centers, or Chakras, within our bodies. If you want to learn more about the meaning of the individual center's colors, body domain and life lesson, there's a chart at the end of the book. I always give the main character in our story the appropriately colored tail feather that their situation centers upon so they can remember me and what they have learned.

Zephyr: *The healing of this chakra re-plugs your energy so that you are vibrating fully.*

Jasper: If you don't understand what Zephyr means then trust me, you will by the end of your story. There you have it. These are stories with a purpose – to reveal the truth and heal your heart. By the way, do you know how cool it would be to your children and grandchildren to have a personalized story about you?

Zephyr: *And since all stories are universal, there is a universal healing for all those readers who have walked your same walk.*

Jasper: That's right. Thanks, Zephyr. If you want to have your story published in our future *Change Your Story, Change Your Life* books, just submit it to the author for consideration. If we select your story we'll change the names to protect your anonymity, and provide your story for our readers' entertainment and insight. Happy writing and get ready for the GOOD that's coming directly to you. Enjoy the following true stories with a friend. Read them aloud and share your own remembrances. Another great way to use this book is by reading it with a child you know. They get to see that adults were once just like them and now they'll have the wisdom of your experience through these wonderful stories.

Love,
Jasper the Joy Bird & Zephyr the Wind

❖

I hope you enjoyed meeting the Power Posse. If you related to Jasper and Zephyr they are there for your journey, too. Hopefully you'll have as much fun bringing them along or creating your own dynamic duo for your personal parable. Enjoy the following stories and I can't wait to read yours.

Chapter Three

Bea Wished
– *Divorce/Abandonment* –

*This is Bea's memory of the loss of her Dad when she was fifteen years old. Her parents divorced at this time. There was little information given as to the reason for the divorce and so Bea was left with confusion and deep sadness. Although as an adult Bea has enjoyed many successes with her career, family and friends, she had difficulty in the area of relationships with men. She is very reticent about sharing her intimate feelings of love with them. She doesn't feel that she chooses the men in her life, but rather they choose her and she goes along with their choice. She does not like conflict in relationships, and therefore avoids sharing honestly her relationship needs and wants. Her relationship history has been that she is involved in lengthy relationships with good men who do not **hear** her or her feelings. She is currently divorced. This is her story.*

One hot summer day Jasper the Joybird was twirling in the hot currents of air that his friend Zephyr the Wind was blowing.

"Hey, Zephyr, knock off the hot breath, you're scorching my tail feathers!"

"No pain, no gain my little fowl friend."

"Oh, here we go with your philosophical messages. Please, just tone down the heat a notch."

Zephyr laughed heartily, which caused a whiff of cool air to circle around Jasper.

Jasper loved nothing better than flying above the earth with Zephyr. He hummed a little tune as they flew over the San Joaquin Valley on their way to Northern California. The farms below looked like a patchwork quilt. They soared over fields of grape vines, cotton crops and several small communities which included a town called Fresno. The heat was stifling.

"Look, Zephyr, there's a pool. I'm making a beeline for it! Can you give me a push?"

Down Jasper flew like a dart towards its target. SPLASH! The water was cool and Jasper submerged himself completely and swam around for awhile. Refreshed, he emerged from the pool, jumped out and shook the water from his cute little glistening body and beautiful rainbow-colored tail feathers.

"Ah, that's what life is all about, Zephyr."

"Simple pleasures are the best," Zephyr agreed as he helped blow dry his little friend.

"That's it. I'm leaving!" yelled an angry man as he got in his black and red Nash Rambler. The car's tires squealed down the driveway. He was gone.

"Wowser, that's not a happy fella. Wonder what ticked him off? Oh well, not our business. Let's get on our way, Zephyr."

Jasper flapped his wings, but he could only get about six inches off the ground.

"Come on, Zephyr, give me a little lift."

"I have a feeling we may not be going anywhere," Zephyr said.

"But I can't help that guy, he's long gone. So puff up and give me one of your best exhales, I want to get to that vineyard up in Santa Rosa before dark."

Zephyr curled himself into a tight spiral, inhaling until it hurt, and then with a full exhale that was packed with exertion, he unleashed himself like a party blow toy. Jasper simultaneously flapped his wings furiously, but to no avail. Depleted, the two friends looked knowingly at each other.

"Our contract with the Universe has been activated, but I don't see anyone around here. Do you, Zephyr?"

"Perhaps the house that the angry man pulled out of could shed some light if we found a window to look into."

The two friends moved closer to the redwood ranch house. It was nestled cozily amongst lush fruit trees. Sure enough they heard someone crying as they got closer. Jasper flew to the top of the nearby bush and peered in the window. He spotted a young girl about fifteen years old sprawled on her bed. She was crying.

"Dad's really gone this time," she wailed.

"Oh, Zephyr, she's really upset. That angry guy must have been her Dad. How could he leave her?"

"Jasper, when the heart is hurt it becomes disconnected from our Truth."

"Zephyr, please speak English, will you?"

"What I mean is that we can't judge him because we don't know what happened to make him behave that way. Clear enough?"

"I guess you're right. I just hate to see someone like her crying this way. She looks like she's in a lot of pain. We've got to help."

Jasper tapped on the window with his beak and the young lady looked up with startled green eyes. Without hesitation she moved to the window and opened it.

"Hi, I'm Jasper, thanks for letting me in. It's hotter than a chili pepper out here!"

He flew to the girl's dresser and settled himself comfortably on top of her music box. She just stared at him in amazement.

"I'm probably a little shocking and that's why you're not talking. Hey, that's a rhyme! I must write these down for future use. What's your name, young lady? By the way you're just too pretty to look so sad."

"My name is Beatrice."

"Well, it's great meeting you, Beatrice. I saw a really angry man ripping out of here in a black and red Nash. Anyone you know?"

"Yeah, that was my Dad." Beatrice lowered her head and

began to cry softly. "They're really getting a divorce this time. He's left us for good." She collapsed back onto her bed.

"Why did he leave?"

"I don't really know. They always argue, but they usually get over it. I hate it when they argue, I get scared. I pray that they will make up. I think they really do love each other, but they argue a lot."

"Are you close to your Dad?"

"Oh, yeah." Beatrice is happier as she tells Jasper more about her relationship. "We've always been really close. My Mom says I'm the apple of his eye. I try to please my Dad because I think he doesn't feel too good about himself. He's a good athlete so I like doing sporty things with him. I try to make Dad feel loved by giving him big hugs, especially when my Mom is giving him the cold shoulder during a fight.

"I think that's great that you are the apple of your Dad's eye, as long as you are loved for who you are, and not what you think you have to be in order to maintain that position. Otherwise you are as trapped as many of my fine feathered friends who reside in a cage."

"You mean the apple becomes the poison apple? I don't think I've ever thought about it like that before. I know I enjoy having my Dad's favor, but I also can see where I have played to my Dad's interests so I would get his favorable attention."

"It's just something to think about because you are loveable just for being you. You also mentioned that you didn't think your Dad feels too good about himself. Is there a reason?"

"I don't know for sure, but I think he feels that my Mom thinks he isn't enough because he didn't go to college like she did. He seems miserable in his job and has a really bad attitude. My Mom keeps trying to help him learn how to get along to get ahead, but he doesn't listen and then they fight some more. I wish I could make him have the perfect job. I wish I could make him happy. I wish I could make them stop arguing. I wish I could get my Mom and Dad back together. I wish... "

Jasper jumps off the dresser and sits on Beatrice's bent knees. Zephyr makes his presence known by offering a cool breeze that rustles the lacy curtains.

"Hi, Beatrice, I'm Zephyr the Wind, Jasper's friend. We've been sent here to help you. There is something I must say to you. If you wish to mend another's strife, you will only wish away your life."

Looking Beatrice squarely in the face, Jasper explains, "Honey, if I carried around as much responsibility for everyone's problems as you do, I would never get off the ground, let alone fly through the clouds. Get this straight, and get it good. You didn't cause your parent's problems or your Dad's anger. You've been trying to fix him and you just can't do that. Do you like Mexican food?"

Quizzically Beatrice looks at Jasper and says, "Yes, why?"

"Because this is a dish you might want to partake in – Nachos, like in Nacho business! What your Dad feels about himself, what job he's in, what makes him happy, is nacho business, get it?"

Zephyr encircles the duet with his soft breeze. "Your heart is burdened with concerns which you have no power to lift. It makes you heavy and hopeless. Are you willing to let us help you lighten your load?"

"Yes, I am!" Beatrice's face is filled with eagerness and anticipation for the wisdom that she trusts these two new friends to deliver.

Zephyr begins, "You carry the weight of your family and their family's past on your shoulders. You can release this heaviness by releasing your belief that you can change others. Changing another person is not within your power. You can only be responsible for you. Your Dad's happiness is not your responsibility. Your Dad's anger belongs to him. You didn't cause it and you won't cure it. Whether your parents choose to work on their marriage and make it succeed is out of your hands. Only they can decide that."

"Gee, Zephyr, I don't feel better. Now, I feel like I have no power at all. You mean I'm just supposed to let go and let my family do whatever they like regardless of how it makes me feel?"

"Beatrice, you have just discovered the power to release your burdens and it has nothing to do with anyone else needing to do anything."

"I have? I don't know what I discovered."

"Feelings. When you said, '...how it makes me feel,' you were talking about something that you do have power over – your feelings. They belong to you and that is your responsibility to share with your family. You have every right to share with your family how their arguing affects you and makes you feel afraid, how you feel about your Dad's leaving and how not knowing why he's left makes you confused, how you feel about their getting a divorce and what you need from them. You can tell your Dad that by not knowing why he left, you feel responsible. Let your Dad hear your feelings. Do not carry this burden. Speak with honesty and tell him how you feel. I caution you to remember, however, you must not think that you can control the outcome after sharing your feelings. But you will have unburdened yourself."

"But I don't want to hurt my Dad's feelings. He will feel badly, I know he will."

"So his feelings are more important than yours?" Zephyr asked.

"I guess so. I'm afraid he might get angry too. It's just easier to wait it out and see what happens. That's what I usually do."

Jasper jumps up and down with absolute frustration. "And exactly how's that working for you? You look to be fifteen years old. At this time of your life you ought to be the center of your family's interests. You are becoming a young woman. You probably are thinking about boyfriends and parties. You ought to have no worries about your family, unless they specifically sit down with you and let you in on the problem and tell you what they need from you. Beatrice, you just can't sit and wait for other people to determine your fate. You have the power of choice. Choose to talk with your Dad – let him know how you feel – what it is you want. If what you fear happens, that he gets hurt or angry, what can you do? Trust that you will take care of yourself even if that is his response.

If he blames you for hurting his feelings, you can explain that wasn't your intention. If he goes ballistic, perhaps it would be better to share your feelings over the phone. It is not okay or in your best interest to just sit on these feelings. They can make your body sick, my love."

Beatrice hops off her bed and her face reflects a new brightness. "Thank you, Jasper and Zephyr; I understand a lot of what you are saying. I am tired of being my Dad's personal cheerleader. I'm tired of being the peacemaker for everyone. I'm tired of just doing what others decide. I'm tired of watching everyone in this family scream and yell like I'm invisible. I am tired of trying to change them so I can feel safe and secure. I feel used. I feel angry. I feel powerless. I feel hopeless. I feel like I'm not going to take this anymore!!!"

Jasper bounces on the bed until he almost hits the ceiling. "Now you're talking, baby! You're feeling the feelings that have been buried for quite awhile. They can get you motivated to make a change right here and right now!   What's it going to be, Beatrice?   Hey, did you know that your name actually sounds like Be Trust, Beatrice?"

"You know, Jasper, I never thought of that before, but I think that's exactly what I need to start doing. Trust myself that I can handle whatever happens after I share my feelings. I can't be afraid of other people's reactions. I have decided that I want to talk to my Dad and let him know what it is I want. I'm going to call him right now!"

"Before you do, Beatrice, I want to give you one of my tail feathers. It is the blue one and it is to remind you that you always have a choice and you must give your feelings voice." Jasper plucks the beautiful feather from his tail and presents it ceremoniously to Beatrice.

"Oh, Jasper, it is so beautiful. I will hold on to it while I make my call."

"You might want to give her a red feather too, Jasper. Let it remind you that you are always safe and you are loveable just the way you are."

"Gees, Zephyr, if I keep listening to you I'm going to end up featherless. Just kidding, I can spare a red tail feather, no problem."

Holding the two feathers in her hand, Beatrice begins to dial the phone. "It's ringing. Hello, Dad?"

Jasper pushes the speaker button and tilts his head for Beatrice's approval. She nods.

"This is Beatrice, Dad. How are you?"

"I'm not doing too well, honey. I've just had it with your Mom. I've tried everything and we're just not going to make it. That woman is impossible."
"Dad, I don't think you heard me. I said this is Beatrice. I'm not Mom. All that you just talked about has to do with you and Mom, not me. I'm sorry you are not doing well. Do you want to know how I am doing?"

Jasper and Zephyr are flying around the bedroom clapping and giving Beatrice the "thumbs up."

"Of course I want to know how you are doing. How are you?"

"I'm feeling awful. I feel abandoned, betrayed, angry and alone. When I heard your car screech out of here today, you don't know the fear that filled my whole body. I wondered what was going to happen to me, to our family. Would I ever see you again? Who would I be living with? Then I talked with some friends and they helped me see that my feelings were important and that I needed to share them with you. I thought I was important to you."

"You are the most important person to me. That's why I couldn't stand to see you before I left. It just hurt too much."

"But, Dad, what did you think about my feelings? You're the parent. Did you think I wasn't capable of feeling anything? Did you think I didn't need any explanation? Did you think of me at all?"

"My God, Beatrice, do you really think I wasn't thinking of you. My heart felt pulled out. How could you think that I didn't think about you?"

Zephyr's soothing voice comes over the speaker phone. "Hi there, I'm a friend of Beatrice's. My name is Zephyr. I know you're Beatrice's Dad but I don't know your name."

"Uh, it's Al. I'm not sure who you are. This is a private conversation."

"It's all right, Dad. It's one of my new friends that I mentioned. They have really helped me a lot."

Zephyr calmly begins, "Al, I know how much pain you are feeling right now. The break up of a relationship hurts in the heart. However, as a parent, we can't forget our children's pain because we are so consumed by our own. Beatrice needs to express how she is feeling and the best you can give her are some straight answers and lots of love and reassurance. I know that you may feel all this in your heart, but she doesn't have a crystal ball, does she?"

"No, Zephyr, I guess she doesn't. I see where I have not been sharing and that Beatrice could interpret that as not caring. Please, honey, give me a chance to answer any and every question you have. I want you to know how much you mean to me."

Jasper flies over to the phone and speaks directly into the mike. "Hey, Al, Jasper here, I'm one of Beatrice's new friends, too – the only mistake you made was just not expressing your feelings and guess what, that's the only mistake that Beatrice made too. She was expecting you to mind read her needs."

"Dad, why don't you come on over so we can talk about when I'm going to see you and I want some say in who and where I'm going to be living. I also want to know if there's enough money to keep living the way we have been or if there's going to be some changes. I also want to know where I can reach you. I understand now that I can't make you and Mom stay together but I can have my input about those things that do affect me. Will you come over, Dad?"

"I'm on my way, honey. Thanks, Jasper and Zephyr, I hope you will still be there when I get there. I owe you two a lot and I would like to thank you in person."

"Al, our work here is finished. We've got a date at a vineyard in Santa Rosa, but just look up in the sky and you will see us. However, I am going to give Beatrice a green feather for you. Let it remind you that when you give from your heart, your actions will reflect the language of love."

Jasper plucks a green feather and gives it to Beatrice.

"Zephyr, here. I just want to say goodbye, Al. You have done a good thing for your daughter. You are clearly expressing your love and valuing her needs. This is going to allow her to re-pair her head with the truth in her heart, that she is perfect, whole and complete. You're a good Dad."

Jasper flies over to Beatrice and sits on her bed. "Well, you have spoken your needs. You let go of needing to change your Dad's behavior and you got what you asked for. You must feel really good inside."

"Beatrice, remember that forgiveness is also the attribute of the green feather, it is part and parcel of love. Your Dad did the best he could with what he had at the time," added Zephyr.

"Thank you both for helping me see all my choices, and that by choosing to sit on my feelings, I wasn't helping myself or my Dad. You arc the most wonderful friends a kid could ever have. And thank you for all your feathers, Jasper."

Jasper and Beatrice hug each other as Zephyr wraps his warm breeze around them. Jasper flies to the window waving goodbye as he flaps, and is easily air lifted by Zephyr's gust of wind. Beatrice rushes to the window and with an upturned face blows her friends a kiss.

Jasper and Zephyr are once again where this story began, in the beautiful blue skies over Fresno. Jasper takes one quick glance back to the road below. His little chest feathers puff up as he sees Al's hand waving from his red and black Nash Rambler as it zips down the road lined with peach trees.

THE END

Since the rewriting of her story, Bea has really found her voice. She is taking more responsibility in standing up for her beliefs and yet allowing others to maintain their point of view. Currently, she has chosen to resume a long time relationship where both participants are committed to treating each other the way they now know they want to be treated. She is also opening up and expressing her loving feelings more freely. For the first time she does not feel trapped by being in a relationship as she now knows she always has choice, and relationship does not have to mean you are tied at the hip. In writing her book, **Change Your Story, Change Your Life***, she wants others to benefit, as she did, from rewriting their stories and experiencing the positive life transformations that can take place.*

If you are going through a divorce right now, these are great questions to ask your children, or if you are a child, ask these of yourself and your parents.

Because divorce is so prevalent in our society I am including these helpful questions at the end of my story, *Bea Wished*.

1) Do you feel responsible for what someone else feels, says or does?

2) Do you think you can change someone other than yourself?

3) Do you ever feel responsible for your parent's problems?

4) Is there something you would like to share with your parents? Will you?

5) Have you shared your feelings over something that bothers you?

6) Is it okay to be angry at a loved one?

7) What keeps you from sharing your feelings with a loved one?

Chapter Four

Ricky No Ticky
– *Dyslexia* –

Richard is a 50 year-old-man. He has had a hard time with finances during his lifetime. He has adult auditory deficit syndrome. He has difficulty reading the fine print on contracts and staying focused on details. This challenge has cost him a lot of time and money. To compensate for his learning disability he usually plays the part of "class clown" or the guy who's way out there.

Jasper the Joybird was soaring in the beautiful powder blue sky. Zephyr the Wind lifted him higher and higher. Jasper stretched his bright blue wings making them longer and longer. Oh how his friend Zephyr and he loved to fly. His friend, the Wind, tickled his rainbow-colored tail feathers.

Suddenly Jasper began to lose elevation. He flapped his wings furiously but there was no chance, he was definitely going down. Jasper used his bright blue eyes to scan the earth which was coming up fast.

He saw a little boy sitting in the corner of his backyard. His knees were tucked into his chest and his head rested upon them. Jasper and Zephyr understood what was happening. Jasper was given the gift of flying, however, whenever there was a wrong that needed to be made right, Jasper would not be able to stay up in the air. He would have to come down to help solve whatever the problem might be. Seeing this little boy all curled in the corner let Jasper know he was being called upon to help. He swooped down and landed on the boy's baseball cap.

"Why so glum, chum?" questioned Jasper.

The little boy looked up in shock. He started swatting at his cap.

"What the heck's on my hat? Get off!" he screamed as he danced around.

"Hey hold your horses. I'm Jasper the Joybird and my friend Zephyr the Wind is around and we're here to help. You look mighty sad and lonely. How come you're not with the kids I saw over there in the field playing baseball?"

"They don't want to play with me. They call me the dummy. I can't read. I'm not smart. They all know I'm in the lowest group at school. They call me Ricky No Ticky. I don't have any friends, so I just watch them and play by myself. It's okay… Hey, how can a bird talk?"

Jasper puffed up his chest and said, "I'm a bird of many talents. The thing I do best is help people solve problems. You don't have to be a good reader to do that, you just have to be a good listener. Come on, Ricky, let's go join the baseball game. Don't be afraid, just follow Zephyr and me."

Jasper and a shy Ricky crossed the street to the big baseball field. One boy hit a pop fly. Jasper sprung into the air, caught the ball and threw it to first base.

"Out!" called the ump.

"Wow!" cheered all the kids. "How in the world did he do that? What a bird!"

Spike, the team captain, came over to Jasper who had landed on Ricky's shoulder.

"That was cool. Is that bird yours, Ricky?"

"Yeah, Ricky and I are best friends," interrupted Jasper.

"Ricky No Ticky has a bird that's tricky," sang one of the kids.

The team laughed in unison.

He's gonna need more than a trick bird to be a part of our group," yelled the bully Butch.

"See you later Ricky, nice bird," commented Spike.

Ricky turned and slowly walked away. "See what I mean, Jasper and Zephyr, they don't want the "dummy" around. I'm going home."

Jasper hovered over Ricky on the slow walk home. "Okay, Ricky, what you need to do is figure out what you're good at," soothed Jasper.

"I can't think of anything I'm good at. I can't read, I'm bad in math and I can't remember what my teacher talks about in class.

"We are all talented, Ricky, sometimes our talents aren't always apparent to us," said Zephyr.

"Okay, okay, I have a full understanding of what you can't do. I want to know what you can do. Do you sing?" asked Jasper.

"No."

"Do you play sports?"

"No not really."

"Do you cook?"

"That's girl stuff."

"Do you build things?"

"Yeah, I'm good at that. As a matter of fact I made a neat bird house. You can use it if you want."

"Now we're cooking," tweeted Jasper happily. "Do you draw?"

"Yeah, I have a cat book that I made drawing 50 different kinds of cats."

"Bingo! We've hit gold. Ricky old buddy, you are a talented kid. Just because you can't read doesn't mean you're not smart."

"Yeah, but teachers don't care if you can draw or build stuff."

"Oh really? Ricky, you need to talk to some architects. I'm not saying reading isn't important, but I think you just need to find someone who can help you learn to read using your style of learning. You probably don't learn best by listening, but probably you like to see things and feel things. There are teachers who know all about that and can really help you out."

"No kidding, Jasper? You really think someone could teach me to read?"

"When the student is ready, the teacher will appear," added Zephyr.

Ricky, Jasper and Zephyr high fived each other. Suddenly the doorbell at Ricky's house began to ring. Ricky ran to get it. It was Spike, the captain of the baseball team.

"Hi, Ricky. I've lost my cat. He's black and white. Have you seen him?"

"No, I haven't, Spike. I'm sorry. Do you have a picture of him? You could put his picture around the neighborhood with your phone number."

"Gee, Ricky, that's a great idea, but I don't have any photos of him."

Jasper landed on Ricky's shoulder and whispered something in his ear. Ricky's face lit up.

"Hey, Spike, I'm a pretty good drawer of cats. If you can describe your cat I could draw a picture of him and you could make copies and put them around."

"Wow, Ricky, you could do that?"

"Yeah, no problem. Let me get my paper and pencils."

The two boys sat down at the table and Ricky went to work drawing exactly what Spike described. Jasper and Zephyr looked on happily.

"I can't believe it, Ricky. That looks exactly like my cat. You're really good."

Spike ran home to make copies and put them up in the neighborhood.

"Gee, Jasper and Zephyr, this has been the best day of my life. It really felt good to be good at something for a change and to help someone, too."

"That's what I'm trying to tell you, Ricky, that there are all kinds of intelligences and we all have our own special kind. When we work together there's no stopping what we can do."

"Let's play catch, Jasper."

"Why not?" Jasper said as he merrily flew out to right field.

After about an hour Spike came running towards Ricky and Jasper screaming, "I found my cat! I put up your drawing at the grocery store and a lady said she picked the cat up because it was stuck in a tree. Gosh, Ricky, you just don't know how grateful I am. I never would have found the cat without you. Thanks!"

Spike put his arm around Ricky's shoulder and Jasper began to hover over the boys' heads.

"I'm glad I could help, Spike. I sure wish I could just read as well as I draw, and then maybe you guys would play with me."

"Listen, Ricky, I apologize for how I've treated you. I'm ashamed of myself. I told my Mom how you drew the picture and stuff and how we all picked on you because you couldn't read. She looked at the cat picture and said she thought you were gifted. She said, 'You tell him that if he wants to read, I'll help him.' My Mom is a special teacher for kids who have trouble with reading. She says the problem is dyslexia. She'll help you if you want."

"As I said, when the student is ready, the teacher will appear," chuckled Zephyr.

"I could learn to read? I'd love to, Spike. This day just keeps getting better and better!"

Jasper felt Zephyr's breeze beneath his beautiful wings and rainbow-colored tail feathers. One yellow feather floated down and Ricky caught it.

"Good catch, Ricky, keep that feather and think of me and also let it remind you of your personal power and self worth. You are wonderful," Jasper said as he and Zephyr rose up into the blue sky.

"Don't go, Jasper, I'll miss you and Zephyr," yelled Ricky.

"We love to fly and one day you'll know why. Be on your way and we will too. Bringing Joy is what we love to do."

Zephyr swept Jasper the Joy bird up towards the white puffy clouds and they flew away with hearts filled with Love.

THE END

Richard has gained a lot of appreciation for his special talents and enjoys being himself. He accepts his focusing disability and just lets others know up front that he has a short attention span. He enjoys working with kids who also have dyslexia.

Chapter Five

Donna, Don't Cry
– *Broken Promises* –

Donna is a woman in her sixties. She was raised by a single mother and always felt she was given the finest clothes, so she looked nice, but never received her mother's attention. Instead, she learned that appearances were what mattered. She has had several unhappy marriages and is now estranged from her mother.

Jasper the Joybird is floating with Zephyr the Wind encircling him. They are happily soaring above the ocean and look down on a ship, the USS Catalina.

"Look at that island with all the boats. They look like little marshmallows outlining the coast. Welcome to Catalina – wow I bet it's a great place to visit!" chirped Jasper. His wings carried him confidently in the gentle currents.

"Hey, Zephyr, my windy friend, how about getting a little stronger and blowing me over to the mainland," requested Jasper.

A strong gust of wind hurdled Jasper forward towards the city of San Pedro. His little feathers were ruffling with each flap of his wings. He looked a little like a supersonic streak in the sky. "How's that for speed, my feathery friend?" asked Zephyr.

"Terrific, Zephyr, look down below there's a big shipyard. The USS Catalina must be the steamer that brings all the people to the island."

"You are not just a pretty bird, you've got some smarts too," chuckled Zephyr.

Jasper and Zephyr have traveled the world together as best friends. They are on a mission to use their inner wisdom and kindness to help others find their long lost song and regain their voices to sing joyfully once again. During their travels, when they happen upon a person having a problem that needs fixing, Jasper can no longer fly. It signals the right time for Jasper and Zephyr to focus, listen and find the perfect healing solution, which they always do.

"Zephyr, push me by all the people waiting to get on the boat. Look at that pretty Mom with the dark hair. What a beautiful little daughter she has. Boy, does she look happy. What a neat thing to do with your kid, a steamer trip to Catalina. I love that good family togetherness. Look, the Dad is meeting them, too. Hey, the Mom sure looks happy – and he really is enjoying that big hug she's giving him. Wait a minute! The little girl is starting to cry – whassup? Let's see if I can sort this out. The Mom is making a phone call and the little girl is really crying now."

Jasper suddenly begins to lose elevation. "Oh, oh something's wrong. Here we go again," exclaimed Jasper as he landed on one of the pier's pilings.

"It seems all is not as it first appears," Zephyr whispered wisely.

"Stop it, Donna. Just DON'T CRY, DONNA! Do you hear

me, DON'T CRY! You can't go with me now because Andy is here," explained the pretty Mom in an irritated tone.

"But you said I could go with you, Mommy. Andy didn't come to our house like he said he would. He didn't pick you up. He lied to you. It's not nice to lie – you taught me that. You said I was going to get to go to Catalina with you – I packed my suitcases with all my favorite clothes and my teddy bear, Maxie. You promised, Mommy, you promised. You can't lie you're not supposed to – you're my Mommy!" The little girl was sobbing.

"I know, I thought he'd stood me up, but Andy is here now and I can't let him get away. We'll do something together later. Now just be a good little girl and DON'T CRY, DONNA. I've called Uncle Johnny and he'll be here in a few minutes to pick you up. Just go over there on that bench and wait with Maxie, and Johnny will be here before you know it."

The Mom turned away from the little girl and walked in a swanky manner towards the handsome man waiting for her. "It's taken care of, darlin'."

"Are you sure she's okay, she seems pretty upset?"

"Hey, she's my daughter, she knows how to deal with disappointment, a chip off the old block, you might say. Well, let's go I'm all yours."

"I'm right behind you, Joanie, and it's a nice one at that," teased Andy. The young couple held each other closely as they walked together down the big ship's loading plank. They made a beautiful picture of two people in love until one broadened the focus to include the little six-year-old girl sitting on the bench, clutching her teddy bear, suitcase beside her, alone with only the memory of broken promises.

"I can't believe this, Zephyr! Is the woman that *heartless* that she could just blow off her daughter like that?"

"More like that *desperate*, don't you think?" replied Zephyr.

"Whatever! Let's go talk to that poor little girl. She needs some cheering up." Jasper and Zephyr encircled Donna with a soft breeze that caused her to raise her head as she looked right into Jasper's eyes.

"Hi there, little one. Your eyes are too pretty to be so red. You look really, really, really, really, (Jasper knocked his head with his wing) sad! Boy, I needed that – I was really, really getting stuck," he laughed.

Jasper perches on a parking meter in front of the girl and is leaning intently towards her. A smile crosses Donna's mouth and amazingly that small movement makes her little face light up as she questioned, "You're a talking bird, are you really real?"

"Jasper the Joybird at your service along with my friend, Zephyr the Wind. He's invisible but you'll feel him around you. What's your name?"

"Donna. What do you want?"

"Well, we're here to help you. We saw what happened to you. We feel how disappointed and hurt you must feel. It's not okay that your Mom left you like she did. It's just not right, no way, no how," Jasper vehemently stated as he stamped his little foot.

"Donna, we don't know why your Mom did what she did, but we do know that it wasn't your fault. You are enough and very loveable – anyone can see that, but your Mom is not seeing with clear eyes," soothed Zephyr.

We don't want you to think that we're abandoning you, too, but we need to talk to your mother. There's your uncle – where is he going to take you?"

"I live with my Mom at my Grandma Madge's house in Compton. He's going to take me there."

"Okay, go to Grandma Marge's and have some hot cocoa, snuggle with your teddy bear in your cozy little bed and we will return very soon," promised Jasper.

"But you don't know how to get to my house. I'm probably never going to see you again. I'm not important to you either."

"Stopparooni, my little Petooni! You have every reason not to believe us, but trust us, we will be at your Grandma's before you go to sleep tonight. Zephyr and I will both be there. I give you my word on my tail feathers, which by the way, I will give to you so you know that I mean business." Donna gently plucked a beautiful green feather from his tail.

Observing this, Zephyr softly whispered, "Ah, green is the healing color of the heart. Good choice, little one."

Donna grudgingly drove off with her uncle in his white Chevy, her head leaning sullenly against the window.

"Well, Zephyr, pack your best breath and sail me off to Catalina, we've got work to do."

"Hold on, Jasper. I agree we have work to do but my hunch is that it's going to fall on deaf ears in Catalina. Donna's Mom, Joanie, is little more than a kid herself. She seems to feel the man in her life is more important that her own daughter, really more important than her own self. She has a whole lot of growing up to do before she can hear what we have to say. I think our time would be better spent telling Donna about the *'SECRET'.*"

"You are absolutely right, Zephyr. Maybe one day Joanie will realize what she missed out on and make her amends to Donna. I totally forgot that not everyone knows about the *'SECRET'*. Let's go to Grandma Madge's pronto."

Zephyr carried Jasper up into the sky as they swiftly left the ocean and traveled inward to Compton. Jasper spotted a little white house with a nice picket fence. "That's it – let's take it down, Zephyr."

Gently, Jasper floated down to the window sill of Donna's room. She immediately knew that they were there as she flung open the window. "You came back, just like you said. I can't believe it."

"Of course, my dear, our word is golden. We've come to let you in on the *'SECRET'.*"

"The *'SECRET'*? What's that?" puzzled Donna.

"Picture the perfect mother, Donna. What would she be like to you?" asked Jasper.

"She would love me, read me stories and walk with me to school. She would tuck me into bed at night. She would always keep her promises to me. She would listen to me and she would tell me that I was the most important person in her world. She would give me lots of hugs and tell me she loves me every day."

Jasper clapped his colorful wings with glee and asked, "Anything else?"

"No, then I would know that I was really important to her and that she loved me. I would feel soooo safe!"

"Well guess what, Donna – right now, inside of you is that perfect parent – who loves you just the way you want to be loved. That person is YOU! So when your Mom disappoints you, know that she is doing the best she can with what she's got right now. Her choices have nothing to do with you. I know you wish she could do it differently, but she can't at this time. So you have to close your eyes and see and feel that wonderful mother within you and put your arms around yourself in a big hug, smile and say out loud three times, *'Wonderful, wonderful, Donna'*. Try it!"

Donna pulled up the sleeves of her oversized sweater, wrapped her arms around herself, closed her big green eyes, smiled and said just what Jasper told her. Her little face truly transformed into a beautiful glow of warmth and well-being.

"Well?" questioned Jasper and Zephyr together.

Donna opened her eyes. "Wonderful, I had the perfect Mom right here in my heart all the time. Maybe later we can teach my Mommy how to do it better."

"Maybe you will, Donna, but right now you know the *'SECRET'* and it will always be there for you. When you feel that wonderful feeling of being loved, you'll know in your heart that the Universe is going to send more love to you. You are a magnet for love and well-being. Well, Zephyr and I must be on our way. Keep my feather and when you become a Mom yourself, pass it on to your kids, and be the Mom to them that you always wanted – that's part of the secret too."

"Keep an open door for your Mom. She might just walk through it one day. Maybe someday you can both still take that trip to Catalina. It's never too late, you know?" counseled Zephyr.

Jasper kissed Donna on her rosy cheek. Zephyr gently mussed her hair and snuggled beneath Jasper's beautiful wings and quickly lifted the joyful bird up into the sunny blue sky.

THE END

Donna, after reading her story, decided to have her sick Mom come to recuperate at her home. She shared her story with her Mom, and though she didn't recall the incident, Donna felt free of the burden of betrayal. In caring for her Mom, she found compassion and forgiveness. She said she has finally accepted that her Mom was doing the best she could at the time. Donna has a happy life filled with grandchildren and is a very loving grandmother with many hobbies and animals. She is filled with gratitude and love.

Chapter Six

Martha Mistooken
– *Wrongfully Accused* –

Martha is a woman in her 50's who has always felt somewhat like a victim to strong willed people. She always felt that she was easily intimidated. This also showed up in the man she married and then divorced. Being a very intelligent woman, she is frustrated in the treatment she receives from others.

Soaring silently in the blueberry-colored sky, was Jasper the Joybird. Flapping his wings furiously, flying higher and higher, he suddenly stopped all action and glided gallantly over the sprawling Los Angeles metropolis.

"Wow, this city is huge! Wish my good friend, Zephyr the Wind, didn't have that emergency down in Florida. He would love the balmy evenings here in Los Angeles. I'll be sure to tell him all about this. Look at the beautiful ocean, and see the hills – I'm going to fly over them and see what's on the other side. This is nice; it looks like a little village. I can see the sign – this is Studio City. Oh, I get it this is where they do TV shows. There's a big studio right over there. I'll be darned, there's a school right down below me. It must be recess. Look at all the kids; they're really having a good time. The sign on those big doors says Oak Tree School. I like it here – so much happiness."

Jasper circled the schoolyard enjoying all the playful

activity, when suddenly, he began to lose altitude. He flapped his wings to no avail. He was definitely losing elevation. This was his destiny. Whenever there was a wrong to be righted he could do nothing but land and offer his aid. As Jasper descended from the sky, he spotted a young six-year-old boy being taunted by other children. Perched on the school's roof he watched closely to determine his mission. The teacher on yard duty marched over to the group and yelled at the children. They all scattered as the little boy sobbed.

"Roger Caswell, who made you cry?" demanded the teacher.

Without lifting his head, Roger waved his hand in any direction. The teacher followed his hand and spotted two little girls.

"You two, come over here right now. Yes, you. What are your names?"

The little girls slowly and fearfully approached the teacher. They looked terrified.

"My name is Martha and she's Marsha," whispered the little six-year-old girl whose big brown eyes were now even bigger and filled with fear.

"Roger, go wash your face. Now you young ladies should be ashamed of yourselves for teasing someone like that. You are very mean little girls!" shouted the teacher.

"But we didn't do anything. Honest," pleaded Martha in a soft but clear voice.

"I don't have time to put up with your nonsense. I know

what I saw. Follow me to the big play yard. You will sit there for the rest of recess. Maybe you'll think twice before you pick on someone again."

The sad little girls obediently followed the teacher to the play yard located on the far side of the school. This was the playground where the big kids played. It was scary and unfamiliar to both of them. They scrunched down together, trying to make themselves smaller and smaller hoping they could just disappear.

As the teacher walked away, Jasper recognized why he had been called. He flew directly to the two little girls and landed on the bench they were sitting on. They were startled and hugged each other as they stared with astonishment at Jasper.

"Don't be afraid, I know a mistake has been made. You weren't teasing Roger Caswell, and we need to make that as clear as a bell. Oh, by the way, I'm Jasper the Joybird, at your service. I couldn't help but notice that you girls were blamed by that teacher for something you didn't do. Martha, I saw that she didn't believe you when you tried to stand up for yourself. How did that make you feel?" quizzed Jasper.

"You are talking! You have beautifully colored tail feathers. I'm so glad you believe us. We were just standing there trying to see what was happening, and then when the teacher came all the kids ran away. Marsha and I were left and the teacher blamed us. I feel like a cloud of dark gloom is filling up inside of me. I'm not going to tell anyone that this happened. I'm so ashamed. I never get into trouble, I try so hard to do everything right and then here I am – and that teacher says I did something bad and I didn't. This would never happen to my friend, Shelly, everyone loves her. I must be a bad person," cried Martha as she buried her face in her little fists.

"Bad girls, shmad girls! Au contraire, my dears. You are perfect little girls who just got 'mistooken'. Simply put, the teacher was wrongo! So you need to set it right. Why do you feel guilty or bad? You didn't make the mistake, the teacher did. No big deal. She just needs you to set her straight."

"Jasper, I tried but she wouldn't listen!" explained Martha emphatically.

"And then, Martha, my favorite un-feathered friend, you just quickly gave up! You were wronged and you just quietly and shamefully took it. That was your only mistake. And now you have to make it right. How do you propose to do that?" queried Jasper as he cheekily jumped onto Martha's little knee.

"I don't know. No one will believe me – not that teacher on yard duty, not my classroom teacher, not my parents, not my friends, no one except for Marsha," pouted Martha.

Jasper flew to the ground in front of the girls and reclined on his back with his feathered head resting on his wings.

"Okey dokey then, just choose to do nothing and enjoy your life of playing it small, not trusting others, envying others' good, never your own, being a victim – need I go on? Girlie, you need to have faith in your own power to overcome wrongs that are done unto you, or you will be other peoples' road kill! That may be a little harsh, but get some chutzpah and shake your tail feathers – oh, you don't have any, do you? Borrow one of mine."

With that, Jasper plucked out a beautifully colored blue tail feather and gave it to Martha. "Use this feather as a reminder that your power is always with you. When you know that, Martha, others will know it too."

Martha appreciatively took the blue feather and stroked it lovingly. "Jasper, this is the most wonderful gift anyone has ever given to me, but you have given me an even better gift – trust in myself. Now I know what I'm going to do."

Just then the teacher on yard duty approached the girls with her hands on her hips and her face set in a stern frown. "You girls are dismissed to your class. I hope you have learned your lesson."

Martha slowly raised herself off the bench, squared her shoulders and tilted her chin upwards until her big brown eyes were looking squarely into the teacher's eyes. Taking a deep breath, she confidently explained, "Excuse me, Ms. Jones, you made a mistake. My friend and I did not tease Roger Caswell. You mistook us for the children who really did it. It is not okay with me to be unfairly punished. I know you were only trying to help, but two wrongs do not make a right, right? I felt very ashamed and afraid sitting here – I began to feel that I had done something wrong even though I knew I hadn't. I started to believe your mistake. Luckily, a friend reminded me with the real Truth – I am innocent – and you were wrong. I would like an apology for me and my friend."

"Well I, I, I'm sure it was you two who I saw. Roger pointed you out. Oh, let's not make a big thing out of this, just go back to your class and forget it," dismissed Ms. Jones as she marched away.

Hopping on Martha's shoulder as they stared after the retreating teacher, Jasper announced, "You don't always get the result you want, little one, but that's not really what's important, is it?"

"No it isn't, Jasper. It would have been nice, but not

necessary. What was important to me was that I stood up for myself. I didn't let someone else do me wrong and get away with it. I trusted and I risked speaking out and up – Ms. Jones is a tall lady – but she wasn't big enough to admit her mistake. I guess that's her smallness – and to think I was prepared to let her smallness make me feel small – cra-a-azy!!!!!!!"

"Wowser! You are one empowered little girl – you won't need my tail feather to remind you of that, so just keep it to remind you of me."

Jasper began to flutter and flap his beautiful wings as his little feet effortlessly lifted off the ground. He quickly gave a sweet little bird peck to both girls and let the celestial currents draw him back to the blueberry-colored sky where once again he would bask in the memory of the Joy revealed in the story of *Martha Mistooken*.

THE END

But really just the beginning…

Since rewriting her story, Martha has sold her home and moved to a new area and started her own business. She had to go through a messy divorce, but she stood up for herself and received a fair settlement. She is active in her community and providing leadership in that role. She is confident that she now has her own best interests at heart.

Chapter Seven

Kristin Quits Resistin'
– Bully/Victim –

Kristin is in her early thirties. She's an actress and does other jobs to support her creative pursuits. She is not married at the time of this story and feels that she operates between over-reacting and being too yielding. She feels frustrated and out of balance.

Kristin could hear her coming down the hall. The terror began to flood her body, starting at the pit of her stomach and making its way through all the channels in her system. Her heart was racing as fast as her fingers were moving, trying to open the lock on her locker. She heard the footsteps stop directly behind her. Kristin could feel the hot breath on her neck and the glare piercing right through her. She felt as though she couldn't move, like her feet were glued to the floor, permanently frozen by the fear pulsating through her veins. BRR R R ING!!!! The five minute bell rang. She had to get to class. She mustered up the courage to turn around and looked squarely into the menacing brown, blue eye-lined eyes of her nemesis, Allison Heber. The girl's beautiful face was highlighted by her dark hair, but at the moment this just added to her sinister presence. Her perfectly painted lips puckered to emit her daily vitriolic missive, "Roach!!"

Kristin looked down and ran, without a word, to her class. She felt humiliated by her own silence but relieved that she had survived one more day of Allison's brutalizing Roach

Approach.

"Whe-e-e-e! This is a beautiful little town," observed Jasper the Joybird. He and his friend, Zephyr the Wind, were floating happily over Fern, Washington. They were playfully and easily soaring in the beautiful sunny blue sky.

"Fern, Washington is a peaceful place. I love the beautiful autumnal colors," Zephyr replied. These two friends were the true experts of simple pleasures. Jasper, with his glistening blue body and beautiful rainbow-colored tail feathers cut a brilliant contrast to the soft pastel blue sky. Zephyr encircled his little friend with a soft breeze that allowed the bird to float easily above the green fields.

This duo, Jasper and Zephyr, loved to play for hours in the sky, soaring peacefully. However, they were given a life contract that whenever there was a human problem to be solved, try as they might, they would lose elevation and have to help solve the problem before they could be on their merry way. A contract was activated over Fern Junior High School on this very beautiful September morning.

"Hey, Zephyr, give me a strong gust so I can fly over that school building."

"I'm blowing as powerfully as I can, Jasper, but you are not staying afloat!"

"You mean I'm losing elevation? You know what that means, Zephyr."

"Oh boy, here comes another adventure," whistled the wind.

"Let's just land on these school steps and take a peek in the hallway." Jasper peered down the hall and announced, "All I see are two good girlfriends coming this way and laughing loudly. There's one girl walking the opposite way. No problem here."

Suddenly the pretty dark haired girl crashed into her very tall girlfriend causing her to career across the hall and slam into the petite blond girl going the other way. The two friends laughed hysterically as the young girl crashed to the floor with her books scattering around her like pieces of a puzzle.

"Whoops, watch out, Tina, you might squash the roach!" taunted the pretty dark haired girl named, Allison Heber. They continued laughing down the hall seemingly very proud of their attack on their classmate.

Jasper swooped down to assist the victimized girl. "Are you OK?" asked Jasper.

The petite blond girl did a double take, recognizing the words came from the colorful little bird.

"Hi there, I just saw what those two girls did to you. What's up with that? Oh, excuse my rudeness; my name is Jasper, what's yours?"

The girl, who was dressed sharply in her sparkling dark blue denim pants with a pink and purple tee shirt, brushed herself off, gathered her books and stood up. "My name is Kristin Wiley. You are a talking bird?"

"Yes, I'm here to help you. You look like a victim of some pretty 'foul' play, no pun on my species intended."

"You got that right. I have been that girl's whipping post

since the beginning of school and I don't even know her. Every morning Allison Heber catches me at my locker and snarls, 'ROACH' at me. Everyday!!!! I just don't even want to come to school anymore. I hate it here. I've asked my older brother, Peter, to tell her that I'm cool. I don't want any problems; I just want to fit in or at least to be left alone. I've got to get to class, but thanks for caring, Jasper." The young girl with her short, blond hair nicely styled in a long tail down her neck turned and ran quickly to her class.

"Well, Jasper, let's go outside and think this one through. Why would two nice looking girls be so mean to a fellow school mate? And why does Kristin take it?" queries Zephyr.

Zephyr and Jasper glide to the outside quad and rest in the branches of a green pine tree.

"We may need to look into Kristin's history to see when she unplugged from her power. Here's our 'Binoculars to the Past'; why don't you have a look?" Zephyr blows the binoculars gently over to Jasper, who picks them up.

"Unplugged from her power? Geesh, Zephyr, you make her sound like an appliance!"

"Sorry, let me be more clear. We need to look back into Kristin's early years and see why she felt others made her feel important or not. In essence, to whom did she give her power? You do know that we're each given our own personal power, right? We can use it, abuse it or give it away. That's the choice of our free will."

"We've been hanging out too long together, Zephyr, I actually followed you on that mind trip."

"Good, there's always hope," mused Zephyr.

"Whatever." Jasper puts the binoculars to his eyes and observes, "I am getting some scenes from the past here. I see a cute little blond girl inquisitively asking her father, Tom, what some words mean."

"Smart little girl," observes Zephyr.

"Yeah, except her Dad just says, 'Look it up in the dictionary'."

"Well, to give him the benefit of the doubt, he probably wants her to do this for herself – that's empowering."

"She's only three years old, Zephyr!!!"

"Blow off that explanation. She wants her Dad's attention, not a dictionary's definition."

Jasper continues, "Let me fast forward. There's her Mom, Julia. She really gets a kick out of Kristin entertaining the family. Yeah, she's getting a lot of attention for being the funny one. Her Mom gives her a heap of love. Peter, her brother, seems to be dubbed the 'smart one'. It's too bad that we get pigeon holed so early in our families."

"You are so right, Jasper. We get labeled and then we become limited to the family's label."

"I'm going to fast forward to our current time. Whoa, what's this? Her Mom's carrying suitcases and she's leaving the house – for good!"

"Where's Kristin? Is she going with her?" inquires Zephyr.

"No, she's not. Wow, Zephyr, can you imagine how she feels? She must feel that the one person who really loved and appreciated her just left, and without taking her. Ouch!! That has just got to make her feel unplugged!" Jasper lowers the binoculars and looks very sad.

"Well done, Jasper. Now we know why Kristin vibrates that energy. She feels no one has time for her. Important people leave her so she must not be very important, not enough."

"I think I would feel that way, too!"

"Exactly! Kristin didn't cause her Mom's need to leave or her Dad's 'do it yourself attitude', and she can't cure them. Neither of those things have anything to do with her."

"You're right, but how do you get a twelve-year-old girl to understand that?" inquired Jasper.

"I think we just have to go down there and start talking, and Kristin will start listening, and we'll see what happens. My hunch is that she has just met her Spiritual teacher."

"Who is it?" puzzled Jasper.

"Allison Heber," confirmed Zephyr.

"What!!! She's the bully in this scene, remember?"

"We attract those who will help us know ourselves better. When Kristin can start resisting her fear and face Allison she will have unplugged her power from others, and re-plugged into her own power source."

"Come on, Zephyr, let's go find her, but let me do the

talking and don't start with the unplug, re-plug stuff, okay?"

"You got it, friend. Remember, the Universe 'sets up' our encounters for our own highest good. So you can see that when Kristin resists her power to stand up against Allison, it is resulting in her abandoning herself in the same way that her family did."

Jasper cocks his head to one side and says, "Lost me! Hey, look down there. Kristin's on the bench underneath us. Let's go." Jasper flies around Kristin's head causing her to laugh and stop what she's doing. He lands on the bench beside her.

"Kristin, where's your Mom?" asked Jasper.

"She's in Manhattan Beach."

"Do you miss her a lot?"

"Oh sure, but we talk."

"Do you feel okay about her leaving?"

"Sure, we had a family meeting and my parents explained everything. My Mom just needs to do her own thing."

"That's great that your parents and you sat down together and talked about it all. I just wondered if you might feel a little – uh – oh, I don't quite know the right words."

"Abandoned, betrayed, diminished?" interjected Zephyr.

"Thanks for sugar coating it there, Zephyr."

Kristin smiles and says, "No, that's okay. I don't think I feel abandoned because I understand that my Mom needed to leave my Dad so that she could find out who she was."

Zephyr encircles Kristin with his cooling breeze, "You have a good understanding of your parent's situation. Your Mom is using her power to self evolve. You have that same power and Allison Heber is giving you the opportunity to tap into it."

Kristin jumps up, passionately stomps her feet and lets Jasper and Zephyr have it, "Allison Heber is nothing but a bully who enjoys terrorizing other people. She doesn't even know me and she hates me. I don't see her giving me an opportunity for anything but hating myself and everything about this school!"

Jasper jumps up and down while clapping his wings frantically. "Now that's what I call powerful!! How about using that same feeling towards dealing with Allison Heber?"

"Excuse me," interrupts Zephyr, "if I can interject something here I would be most grateful. Kristin, one cannot control the outer world. We can only control our inner responses. Your power lies behind your eyes – rather than in front of them. You and Allison are similar."

That last comment brings Kristin right off the bench again. "No way!!!! That really makes me mad, Zephyr. I would never treat another person the way she does."

"I'm glad to hear you say that. That's one way she is your teacher, isn't it? But the way I see you as the same is that you both abuse your power."

Getting impatient, Jasper hops on the ground and pleads, "I hope you cut to the chase shortly, Zephyr, as I think you've not only lost your power but your friggin' mind!"

"Please bear with me just a little longer. Kristin, when Allison calls you a roach, what do you do?"

"I just do nothing and get away."

"How are you feeling when you choose to do that?"

"Afraid."

"That's the point – fear is a violation of your energy of faith."

"Yoo hoo, Zephyr, you're doing it again – too airy fairy," reminds Jasper.

"Okay, thanks, Jasper. I'll be a little more earthly. Allison is abusing her power by bullying you, and you are abusing your power by not using it. You are resisting your faith that you are enough. If your response to Allison is coming from fear – it's not creative and you do the same thing. If your response to Allison is coming from faith, you are creative and you'll do something different. Since you and Allison seem to be stuck in doing the same dance, my hunch is that you are both coming from fear. So Kristin, quit resistin'!!! Clear enough?"

Kristin's face breaks out into a large smile as she says, "I could give you a big hug, Zephyr, if I could see you, but I have faith that you're there so I'll blow you a big kiss. Jasper, may I give you a hug?"

"Can you ever!!! I love hugs and I have something for you, too." He turns around and gives his beautiful tail feathers a tug. He turns back to Kristin holding a beautiful orange tail feather.

"This is my gift to you. Orange is the color of our power in our personal relationships. Keep this to remind you that you have the power at all times."

"And I give you the Truth of this feather – HONOR ONE ANOTHER," offered Zephyr.

Kristin takes the feather and carefully puts it into her backpack and says, "Thank you both for everything." The school bell rings as she gathers her books to leave. She is full of smiles as she waves goodbye to Zephyr and Jasper.

As Kristin reaches her locker she sees Allison Heber approaching. The old terror returns to the pit of her stomach, but something within says, "Don't resist your faith; instead, face the fear."

Like clockwork she hears the toxic expletive, "ROACH!"

With quiet strength, she turns and faces Allison Heber. Kristin breathes deeply and states, "I'm not a roach and you're not a can of Raid – so BUG OFF!" Kristin confidently shuts her locker and walks down the hall.

Allison's jaw drops in disbelief. Jasper, who has gleefully been watching the entire encounter, swoops into the hall and stops in front of the slack jawed girl and gently closes her jaw with his soft wing.

"Better close it or you'll catch a fly!"

Allison's eyes bulge out in response to Jasper's verbalizing.

"Hold on, Allison, I have someone who you have been really bugging. I want to see if she'll talk to you."

He quickly flies down the hall after Kristin. She comes back down the hall and Jasper flags her over.

"Kristin, I believe you have something to say to Allison."

Kristin takes a deep breath and squeezes her orange feather tightly in her hands. "Why do you hate me, Allison? I don't even know you. I would like to be your friend. I think you're really beautiful."

Allison is obviously speechless and very uncomfortable.

Jasper sits on Kristin's shoulder as he speaks to Allison. "You are being reminded of something when you see Kristin. What is it? Are you seeing yourself as a younger new kid on the block?"

With very little emotion, Allison flippantly responds, "I certainly don't see myself in that Roach."

Kristin has finally had enough. "Look, Allison, you don't have to like me, that's your choice. But I will not be abused by you. If you keep doing what you've been doing to me, then I'm going to the principal. Maybe some kid did this to you once and you're just getting back through me. But I'm not going to be the kid that you take this out on. I'm sorry you're so angry, but that has nothing to do with me. That's your issue. So we can be friends or we can just be polite, but the Roach coach has left the building. Get my gist?"

Allison stares at Kristin and stiffly offers her hand. "I'm sorry, I won't be bugging you anymore." She walked past Kristin and continued down the long hall.

Zephyr ruffles Kristin's hair and says, "You were

marvelous, simply marvelous. You used your voice and gave Allison her choice. I am very proud of you."

"Thanks, Zephyr, it really felt so freeing to face this fear and just say, NO MORE!! I actually feel sorry for Allison, she is angry and she doesn't know where to put it. I forgive her, and I see that her attitude has really nothing to do with me."

"Well, Zephyr, I would say that Kristin has quit resistin' and started listenin' to her own powerful voice within."

Jasper swirls up into the beautiful blue sky in response to Zephyr's strong comforting breath as the two friends once again float merrily on their way.

THE END

Since rewriting her story, Kristin has had many wonderful changes in her life. She made amends with her father prior to his passing and she and her Mom live near each other and are very close. She quit resisting the pursuit of a former boyfriend after twelve long years and they were happily wed. She lives with her animals and husband and her acting career has brought her much creative success.

Chapter Eight

Do Be Doriane
– Sibling Rivalry –

Doriane is a fortyish beautiful woman who feels frustrated in her relationships with men and in her career. She always feels that she is not appreciated for being herself and that she's too much of a people pleaser. She was the youngest sibling in her family and her parents, for their own reasons, were not very emotionally available to her. Just being Doriane was not really encouraged.

"Yodel le he hoo, Yodel le he hoo," Jasper the Joybird yodels happily as he floats leisurely in the air currents on an early spring day. His friend, Zephyr the Wind, is playfully keeping his friend effortlessly afloat.

"You know, Zephyr, I've never flown to the east coast before. It's quite beautiful down there in New Jersey."

"Yes, Jasper, Monthill is a nice town. It seems like it's a place where old meets new. Look at that old farmhouse nestled right in the thick of those new houses."

"Oh yeah, I see what street you're looking at. It's probably no coincidence that the name of the street is Echo Hill. The past is merely a memory with the farm as its token – holding so many secrets not spoken. Hey, where did that come from? I'm a pretty good poet," Jasper mused.

"Do you see that horse down there? I wonder what it thinks of all this progress?" queried Zephyr.

"It's probably seen a lot of changes. Look at that new red house right next to it. Do you see all those balloons? They must be getting ready for a birthday party. Let's go down and take a look."

Jasper gracefully swoops down to the window and peers into the house's basement. He sees two teenage girls cleaning the room and decorating it with balloons. A little ten-year-old girl with short, pixie cut brown hair framing her pretty face and beautiful brown eyes is dancing and twirling around the room. She appears delighted with the activities and her body movements are expressing that Joy. She leaps happily around the two other girls.

"Zephyr, those girls are decorating for a birthday party and ten to one it's that little girl's party. Boy is she happy. I just love to see that. Only kids and dogs can show how they feel so effortlessly. She has such a full heart! It makes me happy just watching her. Well, life is good in Monthill, New Jersey. Let's head off to Upstate New York before it's too dark."

"You've got it, my feathered friend. Here's a swift gust that should get you sailing in the right direction."

Zephyr inhales and blows Jasper up high into the air. Jasper stretches his beautiful wings and tucks his rainbow-colored tail feathers to maximize his liftoff. Up he floats. He gently flaps his wings twice and anticipates the usual glide that follows, but instead he begins to lose elevation. He flaps more adamantly, but to no avail. He is definitely going down.

"Wait a minute, Zephyr, there's no problems on this street. I know I lose elevation whenever a person's heart is hurting, but there's nothing wrong here on Echo Hill."

"Well, the Universe makes no mistakes. Let's look around. Maybe it's that old horse at the farm house," Zephyr suggests.

"I thought we were only in charge of humans – but hey – no harm in asking. Let's go see!"

Jasper zooms down and lands on the fence post of the old horse's stall.

"Hi there! Who are you?" asks Jasper.

"I'm a horse, of course!"

"Great, another poet! Got a name?"

"Ginger."

"Is there a problem?"

"Beyond being old and cranky? Not that I'm aware of. Do you know something I don't?"

"No, but I was hoping you could shed a little light on the subject," replied Jasper.

"May I interrupt your repartee, or we could be here all day! Ginger, nice to meet you; I'm Zephyr the Wind and my friend here is Jasper the Joybird. We're here because we have a commitment with the Universe to heal people's hurting hearts and reveal their Truth. Jasper can't fly if we're in the midst of a problem."

"So why are you here talking to me?" Ginger inquired.

"Because Jasper just lost elevation over this area on Echo Hill. We've been next door and there's nothing out of sorts there. A little girl looks to be getting ready for a birthday party and the place is filled with joy. So the only place left for a potential problem looks to be you and this farm. Is there a problem here?"

"Nope. But I think you need to scratch a little deeper below the surface next door. There's a Goldilocks and the three Bears syndrome going on."

Jasper scratches his head with his wing and says, "You're going to need to explain that one. Is that 'animal speak' or what?"

"Hey, don't get uppity with me. You may have only two legs, but you're still a bird, aren't you?"

"That I am, Ginger, and proud of it! I meant no offense, just need you to explain the situation going on next door."

"Okay, here goes. It's Doriane's birthday. She's the little girl with the pixie-do. Her sister, Andie, is cleaning up the house with her friend and getting everything ready for the party."

Zephyr asks "Where are their parents?"

"Mom's a beautiful race horse type, you know, successful model. She's busy running her own race. I don't think hearth and home is her bale of hay. Dad's got a little too close relationship with the watering trough, if you catch my drift... "

"And the sisters?"

"Andie is a pretty little filly. She's five years older than Doriane and does the best she can without any trainer. She's only fifteen – old in horse years, but young in human. Now here comes the 'three bears syndrome'. Doriane is Goldilocks in reverse. She's trying to fit into this stable and be 'just right' – not too small, not too big – 'just right'."

Jasper comments, "Now I'm getting the picture. She's taking her cues from the others in her family. How they see her determines if she feels okay or not. At least Goldilocks, in the original story, was the one deciding what felt "just right" to her, not to others."

"That's my take on it. So you might take a second look at the house next door, as it may be what the Universe sent you here for. And I'm not a poet either, just a horse."

"Thanks, Ginger. You've helped a lot in getting this picture 'just right'."

Jasper and Zephyr fly over to the reddish-colored modern house with its perfectly manicured lawn and professionally placed small trees. They gaze once more through the open basement window. The recreation room is completely decorated. Andie and her friend are placing the snacks on the table as Doriane enters dramatically twirling and turning and singing *It's My Party*.

Andie looks up from her platter of food and roughly commands, "DORIANE, STOP SHOWING OFF!"

The little girl's dancing is brought to an abrupt halt. The joy melts from her face and the redness that flushes from her neck up depicts the embarrassment and shame that she feels. She covers her face with her hands and runs from the room.

"Ouch! That hurt! What's up with that comment, Zephyr?"

"I think Doriane just stepped out of the family's agreed upon role of her."

"What, 'happy' isn't allowed in this family?"

"Happy? Maybe, but openly expressing what you are feeling inside so others can see? My guess – No!"

"So what are you supposed to do, Zephyr – keep your feelings under wrap and everyone guesses what the other guy's thinking or feeling?"

"Exactly! You make like 'Goldilocks in reverse' and try to guess how to be 'just right' for your family of three bears, rather than for yourself."

"But how can you know what 'just right' is for someone if you don't ask? Even more importantly, what if Doriane doesn't like what's 'just right' for someone else because it's not 'just right' for her?"

"Exactly again, Jasper! Her sister obviously hasn't seen this side of Doriane because Doriane has been the good little sister in the shadow, so to speak. Today she was so free and happy that she just claimed the spotlight and stepped beyond her unspoken family role."

"I've got to talk to her. I can't stand seeing that pretty little face so sad."

Doriane is sitting quietly on the staircase with her head buried in her arms. Jasper lands lightly on the bannister.

"Jasper here. Don't be alarmed. I mean no harm."

Doriane looks up at Jasper with eyes registering astonishment but no fear.

"What's going on?"

"I'm Jasper the Joybird and my friend, Zephyr the Wind, is here; invisible, but ever present. We can see and feel your sadness. We saw what just went down. Oh, happy birthday, by the way."

"Thanks, but I don't feel very happy anymore."

"I understand. What your sister said to you was really a party breaker, wasn't it?"

"Yeah, I was just feeling so excited, happy and free. My house was clean, my parents weren't around and my sister was making everything nice for my party. I was so happy, grateful and excited! I was just showing my happiness and BAM! She just blasted my bubble."

"I saw it! I felt awful for you. I'm sorry this happened on your special day."

"Hi, Doriane, I'm Zephyr, the 'invisible one'. When family roles obstruct our joy, we need to free ourselves from their authority over our individual power of choice. Even if it means breaking a long held family role."

"Huh?"

"Let me explain. Does your family express clearly with each other how they are feeling and honor one another for those feelings and the right to have them?"

"No."

"That's what you just did when you were openly expressing your heartfelt happiness. Your sister squashed it with her words probably because that wasn't part of her family picture of you, her little sister. Let's go back in there and help Andie REFRAME your picture."

"What good would that do?"

Jasper pipes in saying, "It might just start something new in your family, Goldilocks. Instead of *you* trying to fit into what your family *thinks* is 'just right' for you, you can teach them what *feels* 'just right' for you. Hey, you could become the *real* model in this family!"

"Doriane, when your sister commanded 'Stop Showing Off' – did it feel like she just told you, 'Don't Be Doriane'?" asked Zephyr.

"Zephyr, you hit it on the head! I felt so ME! I was so in touch with my true feelings at that very moment – so clear – when she hit me with those words and in an instant everything I felt was all wrong!!!"

"I realize we can't know what's going on in another person's head, but I wonder why Andie said that?" puzzled Jasper.

"Only way to find out is to ask," suggested Zephyr. He continued by saying, "Doriane, don't put your faith in your sister's interpretation of who you are – otherwise you become a victim. *Do be* who you are and put your faith there."

"Thanks, Zephyr and Jasper. Now I know what I have to do."

Doriane walks back into the recreation room where Andie is making some final party preparations. Jasper and Zephyr stay by the staircase but the room is still in full view.

"Andie, I need to talk to you."

"Not now, Doriane, can't you see I'm busy doing EVERYTHING for YOUR party?"

Whispering to Zephyr, Jasper says, "Sounds a little like Andie feels she is the victim here, doesn't it?"

"Well, stop doing everything and sit down and listen. I have something I need to clear up with you!"

"Atta girl!!!" Jasper says quietly.

Andie, with a shocked look on her face, slowly obeys and sits down.

"First of all, thank you, Andie, for all the work you've done for my birthday party. You don't know how much that means to me."

"Well, you sure have a funny way of showing it!"

"Yes, you're right. Why would you know what I felt or how I show my feelings because I have always tried to be how I thought my family needed me to be. When I came dancing in here this morning, feeling free happy and light – that was ME! I wasn't *showing off,* I was finally *showing up!!* That was the true Doriane, expressing her true feelings and you just squashed me with three words, 'STOP SHOWING OFF!' That was the last thing I was doing. I'm a little kid who's happy for once and expressing it! Something we don't do around here!"

"Well, I thought you were acting like 'it was all about you'!"

"It was! Is that so bad? Why did you say that to me?"

"You weren't acting like you. You were being 'all that' – a real hot shot!"

"No, I was acting like ME – but it wasn't fitting the picture *you* had of me. So I'm going to REFRAME me for you, okay?"

"Huh?"

"I love you, Andie, but I'm not just 'your little sister'. I'm separate from you. Don't presume to know what I'm feeling, ASK! I'll do the same. If you want something from me, ASK! I'll do the same. If I do something that hurts you, tell me. I'll do the same. Got the picture?"

"You mean the REFRAMED one? Yeah, I do. Thanks, Doriane, I'm sorry. I think we all need a new photo shoot in this family. Hey, little sis, I mean, Doriane, how about a hug?"

"That feels 'just right' to me."

The sisters happily embrace and then Doriane returns to the staircase where Jasper is jumping up and down clapping his wings together.

"You did great! I know that took a lot of courage. I want to give you my red tail feather to remind you of the Oneness you have with your family and yet the need for your separateness, too."

Zephyr adds, "You just shifted how you and your sister are going to relate in all your relationships form now on – it's called the ripple effect."

"Thanks, Jasper and Zephyr. I felt so empowered. I had faith in what I felt. It felt 'just right' for me. You know that took a lot less energy than trying to figure out what's 'just right' for someone else."

"Too much energy can be your clue, when you're in the land of 'No Can Do'! Uh oh, that's my clue to get out of here before the poet thing gets going again," says Zephyr.

"Doriane, you just keep singing, 'Do be, do be Doriane', and it will be number one on the charts."

Jasper and Zephyr give Doriane a big windy hug and then the Dynamic Duo of Good fly out the window and up into the bright blue spring sky. As Jasper soars easily, we hear him yodeling just one last priceless poetic phrase, "Yodel le he hoo, do be do, when the Truth is revealed, the heart is healed, yodel le he hoo, do be do... "

THE END

Currently, Doriane has returned to her former childhood area. She is close to her family and yet has developed healthy boundaries. Her career is now taking off in an area that has always been her passion. She is seeking male relationships where she feels loved for being who she is, just Doriane.

Chapter Nine

Bobby, Who's Business Is It?
– Speaking Up for Yourself –

Bob is 60 years old. He is a successful lawyer and financially comfortable. He has had a quadruple bypass and is very close with his two sons. At the time of this story he was going through a rather bitter divorce. As the younger of two brothers, he remembers feeling that his older brother was favored, especially by his mother. This is a story of a childhood incident that created this belief in Bob. He feels this childhood belief plays out in his adult life as a lack of self confidence and an alienation from his family of origin.

Jasper the Joybird with his beautiful rainbow-colored tail and Zephyr the Wind are flying high in the blue sky. This dynamic duo loves nothing better than to soar high above the earth while admiring the beauty that stretches below them. This is just such a day in autumn.

"Hey, Zephyr, Fort Wayne, Indiana is a nice place. This is a cute neighborhood. I bet all the kids put that vacant lot over there to good use."

"You mean digging for artifacts?"

"Please, kids don't dig for artifacts – they play baseball, geesh, Zephyr, you are really out of touch."

"You may be right, Jasper. I am aloft a lot of the time.

Being that I am the wind, you know."

"Whatever… hey look at that Mom pulling into that white house at the end of the street. Kids must live there. See the nifty swing on the front porch?"

"Yes, that looks fun. I think the Mom has bought Halloween costumes for two kids. You can sure find out a lot just by observing, can't you?"

"Yeah, let's see which costumes she bought. I don't think it's too nosy to look inside through this window, do you?"

"Like it would stop you if I said 'yes'?"

"No, but at least I asked. Blow me down to the window sill, will you, Zephyr?"

"Your wish is my command."

"There's two little boys, must be brothers. Their faces are lit up like pumpkins. They can't wait to see the Halloween costumes their Mom bought them."

"It's funny how we can get excited just watching someone else feeling joyful."

"Zephyr, you're really into this observant thing, aren't you?"

"I guess I am. Sorry if it's ruffling your tail feathers."

"No problem. Oh, the dark haired boy got a cowboy outfit. He's really happy. Let's see what the younger brother gets. Wow, it's an Indian costume."

"Is he excited too?"

"I'm sure he is. Hmm, that's funny. He doesn't look very happy. His brother just told him that now they can be the Lone Ranger and Tonto for Trick or Treat."

"Great idea. How's the little guy doing now – all smiles, I bet?"

"Well, he's turned his back to me, so I can't see his face. I'm sure he's happy too. Well, Zephyr, enough peeping into other people's lives, let's get on our way. Remember, we're supposed to spend Halloween with some friends in New Mexico. Start huffing and puffing and get me high up in the currents. I'm ready to go. I'm flapping my wings, are you blowing, Zephyr? I'm not going anywhere. Hit it, will you?"

"I'm blowing myself inside out, Jasper. Are you flapping your wings or just sitting there letting me do all the work?"

"I am flapping my wings off and I haven't even got my feet off the ground."

"Uh oh, you know what's happening, don't you?"

"What? Your asthma is acting up?"

"No, Jasper, the Universe is activating our Universal contract. Remember, wherever a person's heart is hurting, you lose elevation and can't fly. We are ordained to stay and help the person right the wrong that is happening. It is our destiny before we can be on our way."

"That must be what's happening. You're right, Zephyr. I'm

just not sure what's amiss here. This seems like an all American family in 1948 getting ready for Halloween. Mom comes home after buying her two sons their Halloween costumes. One's a cowboy and the other is an Indian. She gives the older brother the cowboy costume and the younger brother the Indian one. The older brother is happy and he suggests they can go as the Lone Ranger and Tonto. What's wrong with this picture? Nothing."

"Let's follow the little blond brother; you couldn't see his face, remember? Where did he go?"

"I don't know. Let's look in the backyard."

Jasper and Zephyr discover a small narrow area on the side of the house and a small backyard. Jasper hops up onto the fence. He sees the little boy kneeling on the ground playing with his marbles.

"There he is; looks like he's playing marbles by himself. I would think he'd be trying on his costume," says Jasper.

"His face looks pretty darn glum. Well Jasper, we may have just found our reason for being here."

"Yoo hoo, up here. I'm Jasper the Joybird. Can I join you?"

The little boy's face registers shock as his eyes widen and his brow furrows. He looks as if he's ready to throw his marbles and make a beeline back into his house!

"Please, don't be afraid. I'm a friendly bird; I've just been blessed with the gift of the spoken word. And sometimes I can make fabulous rhymes, too. I see you're playing marbles, may

I join you?"

"WWWho are you?" Bobby asks.

"Like I said, I'm Jasper the Joybird, and I have an invisible friend here, Zephyr the Wind. You can't see him, but you can feel him. Say hi, Zephyr."

"Hi there, do you feel the wind in your hair? That's me."

Jasper asks, "What's your name?"

"Bobby. I'm five years old."

"Nice to meet you, Bobby."

"Why are you here?"

"Well, we're not sure, Bobby. We're supposed to help people when they're having a hard time. You know, like when their feelings are hurt. I can't fly until we've discovered the problem and helped the person out. But I don't see any problem here."

"Well, I do!"

"You do, where?" asks Zephyr in a puzzled voice.

"Right here! My Mom just got me an Indian costume and I wanted to be a cowboy like my big brother, Alan, not a dumb old Indian."

"I think we've made contact, Zephyr."

"Right."

"Bobby, what's wrong with being an Indian, especially Tonto?"

"I want to be a cowboy like the Lone Ranger. I'm just the sidekick, not the head guy."

"Did you tell your Mom this?"

"No. She never asked me what I wanted to be. She just gave me the Indian. Alan always gets the best stuff. She likes him better than me. I hate Halloween!"

Bobby jumps up as he throws his marbles on the brown dirt, and they spray erratically around the yard.

"Bobby, you are really angry. Can you help us understand why you think being an Indian is second best to a cowboy?" queries Zephyr.

"Sure, everyone knows that the Lone Ranger is more important than Tonto!"

"That is what you believe, and that is all that is important right now."

"Yeah, I believe that and my Mom never even asked me what I wanted to be. She just wanted Alan to be the cowboy because he's her favorite!"

"Bobby, did you tell your Mom what you just told us?"

"No way! I don't want to get into trouble."

"Sometimes when we *think* we know why someone does something that hurts our feelings, and we don't check it out, we never really know the truth.

Jasper adds, "You see, Bobby, I would feel proud to be Tonto. He was the quiet wise one on that team. I see him and the Lone Ranger as equal. Tonto doesn't have to be the show off – you know, the Big Cheese. He knows his importance as the quiet pal who gives good advice that gets them out of tight spots."

"That reminds me of another team I know, where one is invisible and wise and the other one is… "

"Yeah, yeah, Zephyr, enough of your insight. Bobby, you see I would take it as an honor if my Mom gave me this costume. Except I have prettier feathers than Tonto. Did you see my rainbow-colored tail feathers?"

"Wow, they're pretty, Jasper. But I still think my Mom gave my brother the cowboy costume because she thinks he's better."

"Bobby, I know thinking that must make you feel badly. Where do you feel that feeling in your body? That's a funny question isn't it, but I just wondered."

"I feel it right here in my chest. It feels tight, like a big elephant is sitting on me."

"Do you think you would feel better, Bobby, if we helped you tell your Mom what you're feeling?" suggests Zephyr.

"Maybe, but I'd be scared."

"I don't blame you. Let me show you something with your marbles." Jasper continues, "Draw me two big circles in the dirt."

"Okay, are those big enough?"

"They're perfect. Now draw a 'B' in one circle that will stand for Bobby, and draw an 'M' in the other circle that will stand for Mom."

"Good job on writing your letters, Bobby. You are a smart boy."

"Thanks, Jasper. Now what?"

"Gather up your marbles that you threw all over the yard."

"Okay, I've got them all."

"Now, this is a game called 'Who's Business Is It?'. When I say something to you, you put a marble in your circle if it's your business, and a marble in your Mom's circle if it's her business. Let's start; you'll see what I mean."

Zephyr comments, "Good idea, Jasper, this can save someone a lot of grief. Once we can see when we are in someone else's business, we know we have to check out our thinking."

"Bobby, you wanted to be the Lone Ranger for Halloween. Who's business is that?" asks Jasper"

"Uhhh, my business?"

"Right, very good, put a marble in your circle."

"Your mom bought two Halloween costumes. Who's business is that?"

"My Mom's."

"You're on a roll! Your Mom chose to give you the Indian costume. Who's business?"

"I'm not sure. I think it's my Mom's business."

"You chose exactly right, Bobby, good thinking. Bobby, you want to be a cowboy. Who's business?"

"That's my business. We both have two marbles."

"Good counting. Bobby, you feel second best because your Mom gave you the Indian costume. Who's business?"

"My Mom's?"

"Think again. Bobby, you feel second best. Whose name do you hear?"

"Mine, so it's my business. But I wouldn't feel second best if my Mom hadn't given me the Indian costume."

Zephyr interjects, "Bobby, this is a big mistake that a lot of us make. We feel hurt by believing our own thoughts and blame it on the other person. We think we know what another person is thinking. Bobby, you can **never** know what another person is thinking. You need to ask to find out."

Continuing along with the questions, Jasper asks, "Who's feeling second best?"

"I am. So that's my thinking, I don't know if it's my Mom's, so it's my business."

"You are one smart kid, Bobby. Most adults live their whole life and never get this stuff."

"Thanks, Jasper. So you mean, I'm thinking my Mom thinks I'm second best to my brother, but I don't know that for sure?"

"Exactly! You made yourself feel sad because you believed your thinking."

"But why didn't she give me the cowboy outfit?"

"I don't know. Give Mom another marble because that's her business."

"Why didn't she ask me what I wanted to be for Halloween?"

"I don't know, and again, that's her business."

"I know another marble for Mom."

"If you want your Mom to know what you want to be for Halloween, whose business is it?"

"My business. I'll put a marble in my circle! I didn't even think about telling my Mom what I wanted to be."

"If you had told your Mom, you would have given her the

information that she needed to get you what you wanted. When she got you what she did, you were not happy and chose to believe that she did this because she likes your brother better," suggested Zephyr.

"It may have just been that she did the best she could with no information from you," adds Jasper. "Let's look at the four marbles in your circle. If you take care of your business let's see how you feel afterwards. Ready?"

"Shoot, Jasper."

"Okay. Remember what the first marble was for?"

"Yes, I decided I would like to be the Lone Ranger for Halloween."

"Did you let Mom know that?"

"No."

"First order of Bobby's business is to let other people know what he wants. They might not do what he wants but at least he has done his part."

"Yes, I can easily do that."

"The second marble, what's it for?"

"I don't want to be the Indian."

"Did you say that clearly to your Mom or your brother?"

"No, I just gave up and felt sad and mad inside. I think

that's when I started to feel the elephant on my chest."

"What could you have done to take care of yourself?"

"I could have said, 'Hey, I want the cowboy outfit. Give it to me. Why does Alan get it?'"

"Exactly, Bobby. That's your inner language speaking out," Zephyr comments.

"What he means, Bobby, is you're saying what you really feel and you're asking for what you really want. Of course, you may not get it, but it won't be because you didn't say anything. This is a very important lesson to learn. Now, what's the third marble for?" asks Jasper.

"It was for not understanding why my Mom didn't ask me what I wanted to be for Halloween. That's my business to find out. I can just say, 'Mom, why didn't you ask me what costume I wanted to wear? I want to choose my costume next time'."

"Bobby, you are one sharp kid. You're seeing the power in asking for what you want and finding out what another person is thinking by asking them. With these skills you might become a successful lawyer when you grow up."

"Nah, I'm going to be a professional golfer."

"Well, whatever you choose you will be much happier when you know what's your business and what's not. We have one more marble."

"Oh yeah. My Mom gave me the Indian costume because she thinks I'm second best to Alan."

"The magic way to discover when you are in someone else's business, Bobby, are the words, 'He or She thinks'. Why do you think that's true?"

"Because, like Zephyr said, you can never know what anyone else is thinking, except yourself."

Zephyr commends him by saying, "Bobby, you are one with the Universal Truth."

"How could you say that sentence so it is your business?" asks Jasper.

"I think that my Mom thinks I'm second best because she gave me the Indian costume."

"That's it!! Now you have owned your thinking instead of blaming your Mom for it. How are you going to find out what your Mom was thinking?"

"I'll have to ask her! But that's scaaaaary! She might yell at me or tell Dad."

"You're right, Bobby, that could happen. Is it important enough for you to risk this happening?"

"Yes, it really is. I'd like Mom to know that's how I feel. I guess if she gets mad that is her business, not mine."

Proud of Bobby's newfound understanding, both Jasper and Zephyr cheerfully say, "YOU ARE THE MAN, BOBBY!!!"

"We will go with you, Bobby," suggests Zephyr.

"No, you have helped me so much. I'm not afraid. I'll just take care of my business and you know what? I think the elephant is gone."

"Bobby, I want to give you this green tail feather. It stands for the heart, where love and forgiveness live."

"No, Jasper, I don't want you to lose one of your pretty tail feathers."

"I won't lose it, Bobby, that's one of the Universal Laws. When you give, you also receive. See, I already have another beautiful green tail feather. This one is for you to hold. Remember that loving yourself is taking care of your business. Speaking up for what you want and asking those scary questions and then letting go of how it turns out – because that's not your business – that's God, Great Spirit's business."

Zephyr adds, "Also, forgiving a person like your Mom, when she has hurt your feelings, and understanding that she is doing her best at the time, helps you let go of the elephant on your chest."

"And, Bobby, I think that green feather will look stunning in Tonto's head band, don't you?" muses Jasper.

"Yeah. Thanks Jasper and Zephyr. I didn't know I could learn so much from a game of marbles. I love you both. I feel as light as a feather."

Bobby hugs Jasper as Zephyr's wind gently tussles the boy's blond hair.

"We're on our way, Bobby. Happy Halloween."

Zephyr blows Jasper up into the blue sky as the little bird flaps his wings. He looks down at little Bobby waving from the backyard. Bobby sees Jasper flying higher and higher into the autumn sky. He begins to smile as he faintly hears, "Hi-o Silver and away." Bobby looks down to the two circles drawn in the dust and wonders, "Who was that feathered friend?"

Who's business is it, Bobby?

THE END

Since rewriting his story, Bob has entered into a new relationship and the bitter divorce has finally been put to rest. He feels a new responsibility to himself to ask for what he wants and to listen to his partner's needs as well. He has become much more conscious of not doing to his own two sons what his mother did to him. This story opened up a great dialogue on this very subject after his sons had read it together with their Dad. His health is great.

Chapter Ten

Hard on Richard
– Father's Verbal Abuse –

A self written story by a reader of
Change your Story, Change Your Life.

I always wanted my Dad's approval but I never got it. He had a terrible temper and I was usually the one on the wrong end of that stick. I've spent most of my adult life proving my Dad's opinion of me was right, that I was worthless and I couldn't succeed. I had many jobs; some were good, but eventually I would end up shooting myself in the foot. I was quite arrogant and thought the world owed me a living. I was not the easiest person to live with either. I'm afraid I was too good of a student of my father's rage.

Jasper comes upon a young lad in a small village in New Zealand.

"Richard, now that we have heard all this stuff about your hurt feelings, what could you do with all this?"

"Well, for a bird that is a good question. I could give it all to you, as it is for the birds anyway, right? But I won't go there. What could I do with it? I could relive these thoughts, and then convince myself that after I have heard them and reheard them, I would know what a load of crap these thoughts are. There is nobody there to convince, not even my Mum or Dad are there to tell it to, so I am really just reliving a story that I have personally told to myself, over and over again. If the person is not really there to actually tell the story to, then I am reliving a real fairytale. It is real because I lived the f***ing thing, but it is a fairytale because the actual persons involved have long since gone and no longer care. They will also never know how I feel because I never actually got to tell them how I feel."

"Well, duh! For a human you aren't half bad! So let's take the feathers off so to speak, geez I am a clever bird, and tell this jerk as if he was here. What would you say to his face?" queries Jasper.

"Well, for starters I would cringe because I know what he was like in real life. If I had the chance, I'd have my Dad shut the f*** up, and my Mum would not cry or stop me from talking.

I would say, 'Dad! Just listen to me for 5 minutes, okay? Do not stop me, even if I cry. Don't say men do not do those things, just let me cry, just let me go on. But Dad, I love you. I really love you deep down. I am an integral part of your life. I am your flesh and blood. Half of me is you and the other half is my Mum. I came from your seed and my Mum's womb, and together I make up a combination of you both. I feel that you were very cruel to me in the way you spoke to me. You undermined my confidence in what I could be and what I could become. I had nothing but goodness and love to give you both. I was you in many ways, but I wanted you to honor me for who I was. I felt a big knife being put into my heart when we spoke, and it was twisted back and forth every time you spoke to me. Yet all I had was unconditional love for you because you were my Dad. I can only have one Dad, and you were it. I would have walked over a mile of broken bottles for you, to make you

115

proud of me, and yet I could not even break the bottles to make you proud of me because you would not let me break the bottles.

To be told I am nothing and will never be anything, was saying that you also were nothing, and that you did not mean a thing in this life. But you did mean something to me. You were my Dad, and by golly I loved you for that. I would've loved to have sat on your knee and put my arms around you as we listened to the radio. I would've loved to have you come to just one of my sports meetings. To have heard you yelling me on whilst I was playing would have meant the world to me. But you never came to any of my sports functions. I missed that very much. I really tried to do everything to meet your approval, but I never seemed to be able to match up to what you wanted. And what that was I never had a bloody clue because you never told us what you expected from us. You just yelled and bitched and screamed, and told me I was nothing. Just like a bit of sh*t!! Well, I wasn't. I was your flesh and blood!!'"

"Well, be geppers Richard, you have a lot of love and untold feelings within that body of yours! So just for instance, let's assume that your Dad is here right now, and he has heard every word you have said. What do you think he would say?" asks Jasper.

"He'd probably say, 'Gee son, I thought I was doing the best thing for you. That is the way my Dad taught me, and I believed that I had done a pretty good job in my life. But then again I am not you, and I did not know how you would react. Your brother was okay with it, but I suppose I was taking my frustrations on life out on you. I knew I could be better in life than what I was. I knew I could do better, so I think I really wanted you to be better than me, as you seemed to have the pizzazz to do better. I just thought that you would respond positively to my hardships to you. I never really looked at you. I was just thinking of myself. My Dad was really tough on me, so I never knew anything different. I thought this was the way to treat the son you looked up to. You see you were the last, and we could not have any more kids, so I wanted you to be the best that you could possibly be. You want me to say I love you? Then I will say it in big words: I LOVE YOU, RICHARD. I have always loved you. I am so sorry that my fatherhood has impacted you so heavily. There is nothing I can say but that I am very sorry. Truly sorry, son.'

Well Dad, let me say right here and now, thanks for listening to me. And by the way, just to make your day wherever you are, I LOVE YOU TOO, DAD!"

Since writing this story, I really felt a mental release of the anger I had been carrying towards my Dad all these years. I really never did get to hear those "I love you, son" words that I had longed for, but I somehow could feel what they would feel like after reading my story. Just feeling that nice feeling seemed to shift things inside. I really get that the person who is most important to hear those words from, is myself. When I'm living my life so that at the end of the day I can say, "I love you, Richard," then that brings that warm fuzzy feeling in bucket loads. My job situation has really improved. My lady friend of many years and I have decided to start anew, and I'm really doing my best to do it differently and let the anger die with my Dad's story. I want to be the partner that I wished I had had in my Dad. Life is good.

Chapter Eleven

Now It's Your Turn

As you begin this process of Rewriting your past using your imagination, I would like to present some very famous individuals who have known the power and importance of using our imagination to manifest what we want in our lives. Hopefully, they will give credence to the value of this process. So use it, don't lose it!

The tragedy of life is not death,
but what we let die inside of us while we live.
N. Cousins

Imagination is more important than knowledge.
For knowledge is limited to all we now know and understand,
while imagination embraces the entire world,
and all there ever will be to know and understand.
Albert Einstein

Think left and think right and think low and think high.
Oh, the thinks you can think up if only you try!
Dr. Seuss (Theodor Geisel)

Do not quench your inspiration and your imagination;
do not become the slave of your model.
Vincent van Gogh

Everything you can imagine is real.
Pablo Picasso

We are what we imagine ourselves to be.
Kurt Vonnegut

When patterns are broken, new worlds emerge.
Tuli Kupferberg

Your imagination, my dear fellow, is worth more than you imagine.
Louis Aragon

It's kind of fun to do the impossible.
Walt Disney

Man's mind, once stretched by a new idea,
never regains its original dimensions.
Oliver Wendell Holmes, Jr

The possible's slow fuse is lit by the imagination.
Emily Dickinson

The quality of the imagination is to flow and not to freeze.
Ralph Waldo Emerson

Imagination grows by exercise, and contrary to common belief,
is more powerful in the mature than in the young.
- W. Somerset Maugham

Imagination is not a talent of some men,
but is the health of every man.
Ralph Waldo Emerson

Imagination is the beginning of creation.
You imagine what you desire; you will what you imagine;
and at last you create what you will.
George Bernard Shaw

Imagination is the eye of the soul.
Joseph Joubert

Warm Up Activities –
A Prelude to Rewriting Your Own Story

This is an activity that I used to assist participants to rewrite their story in a workshop. Sometimes you may find it hard to get your conscious mind focused on the past, so this activity of remembering is very helpful and really quite fun. You can do it alone or with others. I've actually done this with friends at a social gathering and we all came away knowing more about each other. So just use it to journey back to memories from your past.

I. Remembering: Stirring the pot of past remembrances

Rules to follow if you should choose to do this activity with others:

<u>Speaker:</u> Share your age at the time this past event took place (estimate if necessary)... and provide a brief description of the event.

<u>Listener:</u> Be present with the sharer, and be honored to hear another's remembrance.

<u>All</u>: What you hear stays here. If you don't want to share, please say, "I choose to pass." It is important to hear your voice.

Close your eyes and playing soft music is nice: If in a group, do all sharing with eyes closed. This helps you stay focused on the past.

Sit in a circle (if in a group) and remember your earliest past memory around the following focal points:

A. Elements: fire, water, air, earth

B. Senses: smell, hearing, taste, feel, sight

C. Emotions: anger, love, embarrassment, sadness, happiness, frustration

II. Writing: This activity can help you get in touch with the emotional impact that the intensity of your writing can conjure up.

You'll write a brief story on one of the following themes from your past:

1. My first memory of getting into trouble.
2. My first memory of a success.
3. My most favorite possession.
4. My first time of really being afraid.
5. My first adventure.
6. My earliest memory.

First write in the past tense as if you are relating the story to a friend. Now rewrite the experience in the present tense first person from your past self's point of view. Following is an example of each to help you understand the concept:

Past tense:

When I was nine years old I dropped a lit match cover into the votive candle receptacle and the heat from the flame caused the glass to burst. I was very ashamed and scared so I ran out of the sanctuary.

Present tense first person:

I want to light a candle for my Mom, but I don't see any matches. I'll just light this match cover from one of the lit candles. Ouch! The heat burned my finger. OOPS! It dropped into the candle. Wow, the candle's on fire, what do I do? CRACK!! Oh no, the glass broke! I'm in big trouble. How could I be so stupid? I've got to get out of here.

Use language appropriate to your age at the time of your story, avoiding present day language if it differs. Did you notice an increased emotional intensity? When rewriting your story, you might want to use this technique of present tense, and coming from your past self's point of view.

III. Internal Language:

Now that your memory has been jarred, let's do some activities to turn up the volume on our inner dialogue. This might be your internal voices that are pretty much going on within our heads all the time. This is sometimes also referred to as the internal mind committee or mind chatter. Let's see if we can clarify and hear the voices that help guide our choices.

You will need paper, markers, crayons or whatever art medium you prefer.

1. You will close your eyes and make a squiggle.

Example:

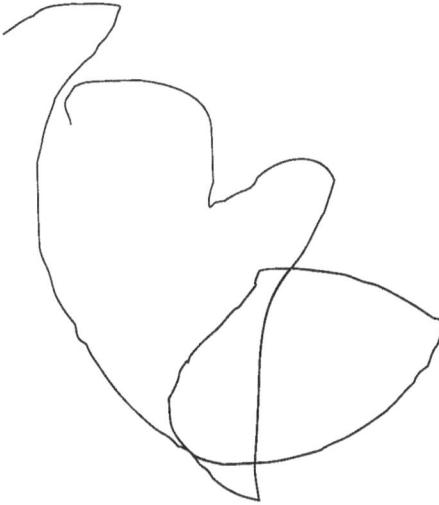

2. Open your eyes. Now close your eyes again and make a second squiggle.

Example:

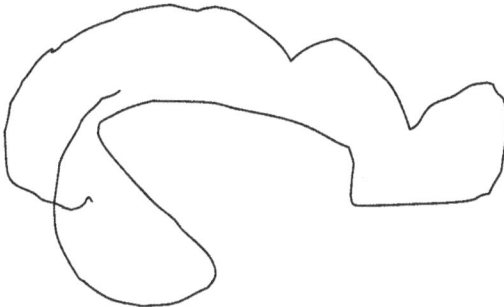

3. Take your art medium and turn your squiggles into two different animals. They do not have to be real animals. Place three numbered blanks under each one

Example:

1. _____   1. _____
2. _____   2. _____
3. _____   3. _____

4. For each animal, write three qualities or characteristics that describe each one.

5. Now describe and write down what you see; pay attention to the colors. Check the Chakra Alignment Appendix to find the colors and their corresponding information.

6. Looking at the animals on your paper, write a dialogue between them; no less than a page and no more than two.

Did you identify a limiting voice? A compassionate one?

This is an exercise in *polarities*, the two parts of your personality. Keep these voices in mind when you rewrite your story. One of your animals is usually representative of the un-empowered voice and the other the more empowered voice.

IV. The Limiting Voice of Your Un-Empowered Past:

Do you have the defining moment that you will be writing about within your parable?

1. Think of the event and write what the limiting voice was saying to your past self to prevent him/her from getting their needs met.

Example: "I'm not going to say anything to that bully. I just want them to leave me alone. Why me?"

2. Close your eyes, breathing in and out calmly and easily. You safely time travel back to your past self and ask, "What am I saying to myself to prevent me from getting my needs met or heard?" You can hear the words, and you write them now...

Now, also ask yourself what it is that your past self wants to have happen in this situation. Write down your past self asking clearly for what her/his need is.

V. Power of Six: Finding the truth of the event

In the first chapter of this book I explained that an event does not generate an outcome, but rather our emotional response, or *our perception*, creates the outcome. We can't change the event in our past for the purpose of our story, but we can re-author our response and the result from that new choice.

A friend of mine is a Native American. She said that her elders, during storytelling gatherings, taught her the technique of the Power of Six in order to flush out the truth, and not allow the mind to justify a belief.

1. You are going to envision your past story event in your mind as you remembered it then.

2. Center yourself, close your eyes, breathing in and out calmly. Begin to time travel back to that time in your life. You are safe. See what your past self remembers happening.

3. Now, I want you to use your imagination and write six other explanations for that same event. Make them up and also include the one you have lived your life by. Can you find any humor in one of your explanations?

In my own story, *Bea Wished*, I wrote the following six statements: 1) Dad left because he was afraid to say anything to me, 2) He had a doctor's appointment and didn't want to be late, 3) He was so angry at Mom he couldn't think of anything else, 4) I wasn't important enough to him, 5) He was so selfish he could only think of his feelings, and 6) He had a hot date and didn't want to be late.

I lived my life with number 4. I can see that number 1 and 3 were probably more likely the truth, and that his actions actually had very little to do with his love for me.

Using this technique of the Power of Six, the Native Americans would say that somewhere between your first interpretation and your sixth lies more of the truth about what really happened. Do you agree?

Was there a shift in your perception or thinking?

❖

Now you have your mind in memory mode. You've identified your internal dialogue and the voice of your empowered and un-empowered past self and expanded your perceptions of the event. You are good to go for rewriting your story. Use the following questionnaire and story prompt to rewrite the event that can be limiting you and really know that you are creating your personal parable for freedom and for future freedom of others in your family. Amazing! Have a special time and remember to share, share, share.

Chapter Twelve

Writing Your Own Personal Parable

Now it's your turn to write your own Personal Parable. Using the following questionnaire and story outline, you will encounter a shift from experiencing a past wound to experiencing the event's wisdom. This memoir can be a keepsake in your family. If you have children or grandchildren, what a treasure it will be to read your story to them. This story may not just heal an old personal hurt within you, but it may also just stop the passing on of this wound to future generations. What a concept!!! LET'S DO IT!!!

Story Questionnaire

Purpose of story questionnaire: Since your subconscious doesn't know the difference between fact or fiction, this remembering of your story will serve to investigate the old negative beliefs of the original story from your past. Using your adult consciousness, you'll discover new, more empowering choices and peaceful feelings. Your purpose is to re-pair your head with the Truth of your heart – which is that you are already whole, perfect and complete. There is no reality, just our perceptions, and the more clear and specific you are in answering these questions, the more real the release of old outlived emotions will be by replacing them with authentic alternatives. The power for change is in your internal responses. You get to CHOOSE again. Try keeping this activity to just one life defining moment. You can use this same questionnaire for all important events in your life, but just take one belief at a time.

Eliminate all opportunities for distraction; this is your time, your internal journey. The information you provide will be used to create your story. Be as specific with details as possible. The richer your description, the more visceral your reaction will be. This isn't an exercise in morbidity, but rather to bring up an incident which led you to create a negative false belief about yourself, and then allow it to be examined by your present adult consciousness via your own personal Power Posse.

Get quiet in a way that is comfortable to you. Know that you are going to give your time to your story. You are going to be reliving external past events, and reworking your internal reactions and consequent choices.

✓ Find a quiet place
✓ Close your eyes
✓ Breathe, allow the memory to rise, knowing you are safe and have already lived through it
✓ Think of a past experience that is quite vivid to you and really hurt you in some way
✓ Ready? Let's go!!!

1. Describe the incident.

2. What would you like to have done differently?

3. Provide information about yourself at the time of the incident:

a) Age
b) Physical description such as eye color, weight, height, hair color, length, style, what were you wearing, etc.
c) Your personality such as bully, victim, shy, precocious, friendly, chip on your shoulder, etc.
d) Name or name you were called by then
e) Your family situation at the time such as parents divorced, sibling problems, what your status was in the family, your birth order, who you were close to ie. parents, grandparents, etc.

4. Information about others:

a) Name of person(s) who were involved in this incident
b) Provide the following information for each person:
   - Physical description (be very specific, as if you were describing a picture)
   - Personality traits
   - Any other pertinent information

5. Location of incident:

a) City and State
b) Season
c) Description of exterior location. For example, if looking down on the location, what would it look like? ie. *A little red house on a street lined with maple trees. No cars on the street, with a school right on the corner.* Describe the location so you feel as though you are there right now.
d) Describe the exact interior location of where the incident took place

6. Incident's effect on you, perform a self-inquiry:

a) What did you feel at the time? Where did you feel this emotional reaction in your body?
b) What did you come to believe about yourself as a result of this incident? Does this belief bring you peace or stress?
   - Is this belief true?
   - How do you act when you believe this thought?
   - If you could not think this thought, or if it was impossible to think it, what would you be like today?
c) How does this belief still play out in your current adult life?
d) What would it take to let go of this past belief? Could you let it go? Would you let it go? When?

7. What are you like now?

a) Current occupation?
b) Dream occupation? What would you love to be doing? Don't be limited by age, education, talent, etc.
c) Any illnesses? What is your physical weak spot? ie. back, pneumonia, etc. What illnesses, if any, did you experience in the past?

8. Important relationships: Important or significant relationships are referred to as: 1) spouse or significant other, 2) children, 3) siblings, 4) parents, etc. Rate your level of satisfaction in your significant relationships by using the following:

a) very satisfied
b) satisfied
c) unsatisfactory

If unsatisfactory, explain what you would like to change.

9. Present attitude:

    a) On a scale of 1 to 10, with 10 being the best, how happy are you with all areas of your life right now?

    b) What would need to change to make this rating higher?

You will be using the information you provided from the above questions when writing your very own personal parable with the assistance of the following storyline.

Great Work!

❖

Materials needed: Have your replies to the questionnaire available for reference. If you wrote on the computer, continue using it. If you prefer to write by hand, have a journal or notebook ready.

State of mind: Quiet yourself in a way that is comfortable for you. Understand that you are going to devote time to your story. You are going to be reliving the external past events, and reworking your internal reactions and consequent choices. Eliminate all opportunities for distraction; this is your time, your story. It is not necessary to write the whole story in one sitting, so just let your inner voice guide you. If you need a break, take one. Trust that you will come back to it.

Story characters and their roles: *Jasper*: This bird with the rainbow-colored tail feathers is the voice of practical choices. He is a master of problem solving. Let him give choices to your past self that you didn't know you had. He is your advocate and wants to help you right the wrongs done to you. He is also funny and witty. Let him nurture you and use the words you would have loved to have heard. He will give you one of his tail feathers at the end of the story that correlates with the respective chakra depicted in the story.

Zephyr: This invisible friend, the wind, provides wisdom for you to garnish from the external event. Zephyr provides the spiritual perceptions to your past events. Let him express your favorite affirmations and sayings. Let Zephyr inspire your past self by ripping away the false self perceptions. He will tell you the chakra energy system that was blocked by your emotional hurt, and the positive affirmations and lessons needed to re-plug the flow.

You: You are the main character in this story. You will be describing, in detail, all the events of this external happening. You will introduce us to the other characters in your story. You will make us feel what you felt internally as your past self. Coached by Jasper and Zephyr, you will have your past self choose a healthier, happier and more empowering ending. You will be reliving this event with the mind of your present self, which can heal your heart in the past.

Option: If you have other favorite imaginary characters that can serve the same purposes, by all means recast Jasper and Zephyr with them. You are the fully conscious writer and director of this story!

❖

A. Story format: Let's do it! Establishing an exterior shot: Every story begins with our dynamic duo of good, Jasper and Zephyr, floating and frolicking in their favorite place, the bright blue sky. Suddenly, Jasper, despite the valiant efforts of Zephyr, begins to loose elevation. He's going down. This is

133

what happens whenever they come upon a person's hurting heart. Their contract with the Universe to rewrite a wrong is activated.

Begin by writing this aerial shot now, and what these two characters see that brings them down to earth. Take particular care in describing the outside location, buildings, etc. Make it real!

B. Situation description & emotional expression: Now it's time to describe *you* as your past self in this situation. What you look like, what you are wearing, your emotional state, etc. Are you alone or with other story characters? If it is the latter, describe them and what they are doing. If you want the scene to start unfolding now, describe it vividly.

Jasper: Let Jasper join you now, once you are by yourself, and have him wittily introduce himself to you. Describe your surprise in being confronted by a talking bird. He will ask you, "What's going on?" Describe the external event, but especially the internal reactions that you are experiencing and believing about yourself.

Zephyr: Zephyr the Wind, who is invisible, gets introduced by Jasper at this point; have his presence made visible to your child.

You: You now trust this duo and let all your feelings out, which had previously remained unexpressed. Let it rip. Cry and shout out all your hurts and toxic thoughts. Let your negative internal dialogue out, i.e. "I never do anything right, I'm stupid, hopeless… " you get the picture, right?

C. Loving support: Now have the duo comfort your past self. Think of all the things you would have loved to have had said to you at that time. Have them say those same loving and compassionate things to you now, ie. "You must feel so hurt by his words?" "You don't deserve this. I am so angry for you!!!" Keep writing until you really FEEL understood and cared for.

Jasper: He usually gets quite indignant that anyone could do this to you. He encourages your righteous anger and wants you to express it. He's your cheerleader!

Zephyr: He likes to impart some wisdom about the event and perpetrator, and that things aren't always as they appear. He points out that your past self is not to blame. Any wise thoughts that help your past self to understand their worth is helpful, ie. "You are a loving expression of your beautiful heart, and this situation is probably causing you to forget that."

D. The challenge: In this part of your story, Jasper and Zephyr are going to challenge the beliefs you have about yourself. They are going to ask you to defend, let go and replace the negative labels that you attribute to yourself.

Fact or fiction?

Jasper: This is where he helps you separate *fact from fiction*. He is going to ask you if you would believe the same things about your friend as you believe about yourself, if you were watching this same story happen to a friend of yours. Are your self belief labels absolutely accurate? If your external event made your past self feel that you are not responsible, would you believe the same thing of a friend who was experiencing the same situation? Remember, use your present day adult wisdom to evaluate the truth of your past beliefs. Jasper is providing your past self with the opportunity to see how limited your internal responses were at the time.

135

Zephyr: It will be calming as you listen to this dialogue. Now he is ready to ask you to counter your negative beliefs with the exact opposite belief. For example, if the external event made you feel that you are always irresponsible, Zephyr is going to ask you to tell him when you did something responsible. Tell him another time you did something responsible. If you played the role of judge instead of the person in your story, you would label yourself responsible, right? Zephyr will lead you to see that another person's opinion does not make you become that opinion. You have choice. You will test their opinion against this new evaluation to determine if it is true or false. You are responsible; yes, you may make mistakes, but you can do better and are constantly working to improve yourself. Let your past self really feel this realization. He or she is not to be seen only by past mistakes, but rather remains perfect, whole and complete.

You: In your story, your past self really understands that he or she must evaluate the self beliefs and labels against this challenge. Is this always true of you? If not, it is not your Truth. Let your child have an *"aha"* moment.

How does believing this make you feel?

Jasper: He is going to ask you how thinking of yourself in this negative way makes you feel. Do you feel happy, proud, peaceful, loving? He will counter any justification on your part as to why you still feel you should believe this about yourself.

You: You will tell Jasper how this incident makes you feel about yourself and if these feelings serve your best interest. Really get in touch with how attached you are to believing this negative dialogue. He's going to ask you what it would take to make you give up these feelings. When will you let them go?

Are these thoughts making you feel sick?
Where do you feel these emotions in your body?

Zephyr: He will explain how, many times, our hurts are held in our body and we lose our energy in that section. Look at the Chakra Alignment Chart in the Appendix and determine which chakra(s) have been unplugged by these negative beliefs or experiences. Zephyr will ask you what illnesses you may have had in your past. You may wish to consult Louise Hay's book, *Heal Your Body*, and let Zephyr state the mental cause and positive affirmation. See what your body was telling you at that time in your life. Are the thoughts that you've been holding on to bringing harmony and peace to your body and mind? I highly recommend acquiring Louise Hay's book as it is excellent for mind/body ailments with positive healing affirmations.

You: Feel free to ask any questions you may have about chakras and let Zephyr answer. You will recall where, in your body, you were frequently ill in the past. Zephyr will give you the mental cause, lesson and affirmation to re-plug your energy. For example, if one part of your body was plugged into an electrical socket and you let someone else's opinion unplug you, you would lose the power from that body energy system. This area will determine the color of the feather(s) that Jasper will give you at the end of the story, or wherever you want it to come in your story.

What is your goal – what do you want?

Jasper: He will ask you what your goal is. You may want respect from your friends, family, etc. He will ask you if you continue to believe this negative belief, and if believing it will bring you closer to your goal? Is your attitude keeping you stuck in a situation that you don't want to be in?

You: Tell Jasper what you really want to have happen to your past self. You'll let him know what you want from others and how you want to feel about yourself. Get excited about discovering that you in fact have all the power you need to not only change your past perceptions, but also your present and future circumstances.

E. Action: Now it's time for ACTION. What do you want to change by rewriting your story? This is where you spell it out and GO FOR IT!!! Tell Jasper what you want to do, who you want to talk to, what you want to say! This is your turn, with Jasper and Zephyr there to assist you in this action. If they need to prepare the way for you, or if they just need to be on the sidelines cheering you on, that's up to you. Cast them in whatever role you need them to play. Write until you feel complete, empowered and peaceful with your dealings; with the external situation and the internal emotional choices that you are re-choosing. Use your alternative positive attitudes here. Have Jasper and Zephyr celebrate you and your new choices and beliefs. This would also be a nice place for the feather ceremony. This is the ending you always wished you could have experienced. VIVIDLY WRITE THIS SO YOUR HEART FEELS IT – ENJOY!!!

F. Ending: Now it is time to say goodbye and let your friends, Jasper and Zephyr, return to the bright blue sky. Impart some wisdom that you have learned from this experience, what lesson or gift you've taken away and will cherish. State your gratitude to this dedicated duo, hug, cuddle, get the warm fuzzies flowing.

Congratulations, you have just taken the 12-inch trip from your head to your heart. Remember to derive much Joy from the journey. This may seem like the end, but really, it is only the beginning.

The present: As your present day adult self, is there any ritual or action that you feel you still need to do to let go of any *unfinished stuff* and move towards **forgiveness**? Remember, forgiveness has nothing to do with the other person, but rather is completely for your own alignment and empowerment of your body, mind and heart.

Suggestions: 1) Do you need to speak to the person who was in your story to clarify your feelings?, 2) Do you want to write a letter and send it? or not send it? or burn it?, 3) If the antagonist in your story is deceased, do you need to visit their gravesite and read your letter or your story out loud?

Do whatever it takes to close the chapter; it is done.

Remember that you are perfect just the way you are; have been and always will be. Your *choices* bring you closer to your Truth or take you farther away. You just made a great choice by rewriting your story. Pay attention in the next few months regarding positive changes in your life. Write them down, there will be many!!!

Lastly, if you would like to submit your story to be considered for the next *Change Your Story, Change Your Life* book, please submit it through the following web site:

www.bornlearnersschool.com

If your story is selected, you will be contacted and granted a writer's byline, if desired, and you will be a published writer!!! Should your story be selected, we'll change the names to protect your anonymity, if desired, and provide your story for our readers' entertainment and insight.

Whether you submit your story or not, Jasper and Zephyr have only one request of you – please share your story with a child. While you are remembering your past, a child may be living it. Please share your Wisdom and Joy.

Appendix

Chakra Alignment

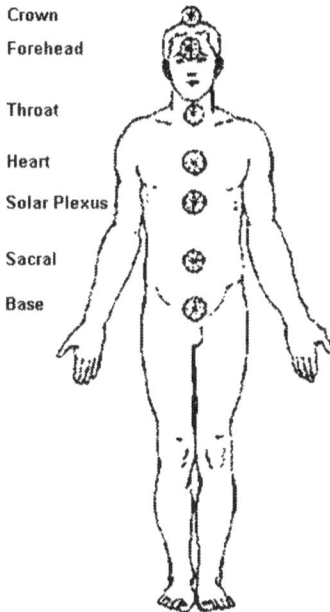

Crown
Forehead

Throat

Heart

Solar Plexus

Sacral

Base

The Seven Major Chakras

	First	Second	Third	Fourth	Fifth	Sixth	Seventh
Location	Base of spine	Midway between pubic bone and navel	Between base of sternum and navel	Center of the heart	Throat	"Third eye"	Top of your head
Associated Color	Red	Orange	Yellow	Green	Blue	Indigo	Violet
Associated Emotion	Stability and security	Sexuality and creativity	Personal power and self-esteem	Love and nurture	Communication and self-expression	Inspiration, intuition and insight	Liberation and spirituality
Associated Gland	Endocrine	Ovaries	Adrenal	Thymus	Thyroid	Pituitary	Pineal
Associated Organs and Body Parts	Large intestine, rectum, hips and thighs	Reproductive system, kidneys and bladder	Liver, pancreas, gall bladder, spleen, small intestine and stomach	Heart, lungs and breasts	Throat, trachea and vocal cords	Eyes, ears and sinuses	Brain (especially hypothalamus)
When Balanced	Centeredness, survival, security, personal safety, grounded	Patience, endurance, self-confidence and well-being	Personal power, self-motivation, decisions, willfulness and self-image	Compassion, acceptance, love, fulfillment and forgiveness	Communication, self-expression, creativity, speaking your feelings and inspiration	Intellectual and psychic abilities/inner vision, visualization, imagination, intuition, projection and perception	Universal energy, cosmic consciousness, cosmic love, enlightenment and spiritual awareness of the meaning of life

	First	Second	Third	Fourth	Fifth	Sixth	Seventh
When out of balance	Self-indulgence, self-centeredness, insecurity, instability, grief or depression	Frustration, anxiety, fear, frigidness and over-sexed	Powerlessness, greed, low self-esteem, doubt, anger, guilt and aggression	Loneliness, insensitivity, emotionally closed, passivity, sadness and overly selfless	Stagnation, obsession and lack of expression or communication	Difficulty focusing in life, detachment, intellectual stagnation and fuzzy thinking	Confinement and closed-mindedness
Health effects	Hemorrhoids, constipation and sciatica	Fertility problems, menstruation problems, menopause difficulties and kidney or bladder problems	Diabetes, ulcers, poor digestion, jaundice, hepatitis, hypoglycemia and gall stones	Benign breast disease, lung disease, stroke, immune-related diseases, high blood pressure, heart disease and arthritis	Sore throat, laryngitis, stutter and thyroid problems	Eye diseases, hearing loss, schizophrenia and headaches	Depression, insanity, psychosis, epilepsy, brain tumors and cranial pressure

About the Author

Beatrice Elliott has her B.A. and Credentials in Speech Pathology and Audiology from San Jose State University. She has her M.S. in School Management and Administration from Pepperdine University. She is also a Licensed Practitioner in the Church of Religious Science. Her first book, *Perfect Praying: 5 Simple Steps that Make Prayers Work*, was co-authored with Jon William Lopez.

Each phase of her career experience has contributed in the writing of this, her second book. The analogy of a seed being planted, nurtured and bringing forth a beautiful flower seems appropriate to describe this process.

Ms. Elliott was a Speech Therapist in the public school system for ten years. It was while working with children who were struggling to survive in the traditional classroom, that she discovered her interest in identifying children's different learning styles. As a therapist, she would test her students to determine their brain's thinking processes. She knew that practicing skills created new neural pathways for learning success. These academically challenged students responded to learning when it was presented as a game or in stories. Desiring more creativity for her teaching approach, the seed was planted for starting her own school for young children. Ms. Elliott started *Born Learners School* (www.bornlearnersschool.com) in 1979. It focused on creating a curriculum that affected the whole child, ages 3-6 years. She began to create lessons that dealt not only with academics but also social skills, problem solving and character development. She was impressed with how great these young students problem solved when they became aware of their choices. Her school has thrived for 27 years in Agoura, California.

Water was poured on this seed and Ms. Elliott wrote and produced a video, *Choosing a Quality Preschool*, which included a book which parents could use to assist them in evaluating and comparing their school choices. This video is available to you upon request. She was also interviewed by the NBC morning show on this subject. Being a Director of her school, Ms. Elliott served as a resource to her school's families on the subject of parenting. She recognized that many were operating without a manual and were feeling ineffective in this vital area of raising a child. Now a little sunshine was focused on the seed, as she began writing a column for the local newspaper entitled *SOS: Seeing the Other Side*. It was an advice column for both parents and children. The purpose was to create mutual understanding between these two sectors. After the success of this column, Ms. Elliott took the same concept to Cable TV. She produced and was the host of a Parent/Kids Advice Segment on the local news program.

In 1995, Ms. Elliott was diagnosed with Breast Cancer. Although a shocking and fear striking event, it was actually the budding of this plant. She had begun her studies to become a Practitioner, Spiritual Counselor, in the Church of Religious Science. She used the tools of the church, positive mental beliefs, meditation, prayer and going to a Practitioner to navigate through this life crises or turning point. She chose to combine western medicine and alternative therapy in her treatment. An energy healer felt the cancer in the right breast had something to do with an emotional hurt with her father. The flower began to grow additional buds. As a Practitioner, Ms. Elliott assists her clients to discover the negative mental cause that is out-picturing in their life.

She began to identify with her own false perceptions around her parent's divorce and father abandonment issues. Ms. Elliott decided that just as she had a hurtful past remembrance, so did all adults. The idea came to her to re-write this memory with the help of a Joyful bird and a Wise wind, and give it a happier, more empowering ending. She remembered the success of storytelling with those challenged students, oh so many years ago. She realized that using the right brain might be a fun way of letting go of old worn out belief systems and replacing them with new life enhancing ones. The flower burst forth into this book, *Change Your Story, Change Your Life: Rewrite the Past and Live an Empowered Now!*

Beatrice Elliott may be contacted directly through her Born Learners School web site: www.bornlearnersschool.com